The MONOCLE
Travel Guide Series

1

London

For more information, please visit *gestalten.com*

————

Bibliographic information published by the Deutsche Nationalbibliothek: The Deutsche Nationalbibliothek lists this publication in the Deutsche National-bibliografie; detailed bibliographic data are available online at *dnb.d-nb.de*

This book was printed on paper certified by the FSC®

Monocle editor in chief: *Tyler Brûlé*
Monocle editor: *Andrew Tuck*
Series editor: *Nelly Gocheva*

————

Designed by *Monocle*
Proofreading by *Monocle*
Typeset in *Plantin & Helvetica*

————

Printed by *Offsetdruckerei Grammlich, Pliezhausen*

Made in Germany

Published by *Gestalten*, Berlin 2015
ISBN 978-3-89955-573-8

2nd printing, 2015

Welcome
—— London in your pocket

Covering the world with a network of bureaux in *New York, Toronto, Zürich, Hong Kong, Istanbul, Tokyo* and *Singapore,* and more than 30 dedicated correspondents around the world based from *Bangkok to Bogotá, São Paulo to Stockholm,* the MONOCLE team knows a thing or two about what makes a fine city tick, especially when the city in question is home to our headquarters: *London.*

From great examples of urban design to smart hotels, bars and restaurants – our London team of editors and on-the-road reporters have put together a list of their favourite places in the capital. Where to take a visiting acquaintance for a *late-night cocktail*? What are the best venues for dipping into the *art world*? The following pages will answer these queries and more. From the ideal route for an early morning run to the top spots for *independent retail,* this travel guide is for those of you who are coming to the city for a few days – for holiday or work – and want to get the most out of your stay while feeling like locals rather than tourists (sorry, you won't find Madame Tussauds in here).

Expect a mix of experiences dotted with some quirky surprises; *grand hotels* appear alongside *family-owned bistros* and internationally *renowned galleries* sit next to unassuming *indie clubs* that play host to top music talent. This book is for those who want to mix the classic with the contemporary, go beyond the conventional and discover all the *hidden gems* that this fine city has to offer.

Welcome to London. — (M)

Contents
—— Navigating the city

Use the key below to help navigate the guide section by section.

- Hotels
- **F** Food and drink
- **R** Retail
- **T** Things we'd buy
- **E** Essays
- **C** Culture
- **D** Design and architecture
- **S** Sport and fitness
- **W** Walks

093 —— 105
Culture
The whole world's a stage but London leads the way when it comes to cultural output. Whether you're into blockbuster exhibitions, gritty garage rock or merely want a comfy seat from which to watch new cinema releases, our guide to the city's cultural hotspots will prove indispensible.

106 —— 121
Design and architecture
As you traverse the capital you'll notice that everywhere you look there is groundbreaking, show-stealing, game-changing design. From signage to cemeteries, stamp shops to office blocks, via some of the most iconic buildings in the world, here's the back story on the city's aesthetic highlights.

122 —— 127
Sport and fitness
Don't let a city break get in the way of your fitness regime. We've put the leg work into rounding up the best places in the city for breaking a sweat, be it in a gym, on a court, along the tarmac or in the pool. Plus: all the finest grooming emporiums to keep you looking the part.

128 —— 137
Walks
One of the best ways to get to grips with a city is by hitting the streets. But where to start? We visit five of the city's most innovative, diverse and interesting neighbourhoods to highlight an enlightening route through the best that each area has to offer.

138 —— 139
Resources
Be in the know with our bite-size guide to the events, the slang and the city soundtrack, plus hints on what to do on a rainy day in the capital.

140 —— 141
About Monocle
Find out more about our global brand from groundbreaking print, radio, online and film output through to our cafés and shops.

142 —— 143
Acknowledgements
The people who put this guide together: writers, photographers, researchers and all the rest.

Map
—— The city at a glance

There are 32 boroughs in London spread across nine travel zones. In fact, there are 33 if you count the City; as the founding heart of London in the 1st century and today's financial centre, it has kept special administrative status as a city in its own right.

From wealthy Chelsea and Kensington to bohemian Islington via classy Westminster, we outline the inner boroughs and main areas in central London. That essentially means zones 1 and 2 on the Underground map as a short visit to London rarely requires you to venture further out unless en route to one of the city's international airports.

We'll leave it to you to judge the debate over whether west is better than east (or, indeed, north superior to south). But one thing is for sure: each of the areas on our map has an embarrassment of riches to make you yearn to return and explore even further.

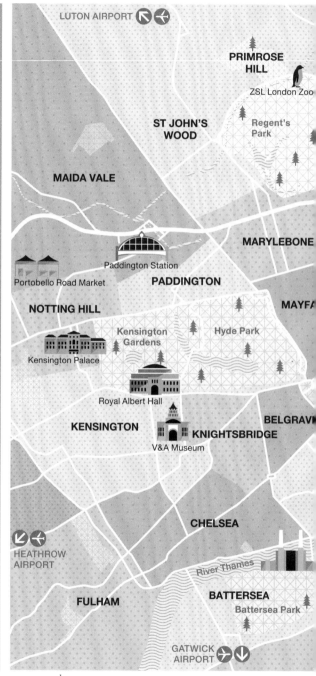

LUTON AIRPORT

PRIMROSE HILL

ZSL London Zoo

ST JOHN'S WOOD

Regent's Park

MAIDA VALE

MARYLEBONE

Paddington Station

Portobello Road Market

PADDINGTON

MAYFA

NOTTING HILL

Kensington Gardens

Hyde Park

Kensington Palace

Royal Albert Hall

KENSINGTON

V&A Museum

KNIGHTSBRIDGE

BELGRAV

CHELSEA

HEATHROW AIRPORT

River Thames

FULHAM

BATTERSEA

Battersea Park

GATWICK AIRPORT

AMDEN
TOWN

ISLINGTON

STANSTED
AIRPORT

DALSTON

ANGEL

St Pancras International
Station

SHOREDITCH

Columbia Road
Flower Market

KING'S
CROSS

CLERKENWELL

BETHNAL
GREEN

BLOOMSBURY

FARRINGDON

SPITALFIELDS

TZROVIA

The British
Museum

HOLBORN

CITY

The Gherkin

SOHO

COVENT
GARDEN

St Paul's Cathedral

WHITE-
CHAPEL

River Thames

Tate Modern

PICCADILLY

WAPPING

en
rk

St James's
Park

Borough
Market

Tower Bridge

BOROUGH MARKET

Buckingham
Palace

Big Ben

SOUTH BANK

WESTMINSTER

BERMONDSEY

Tate Britain

LAMBETH

SOUTHWARK

LONDON CITY
AIRPORT

MLICO

ation

Burgess Park

KENNINGTON

CAMBERWELL

0   500m

Need to know
—— Get to grips with the basics

Discover how to find your way around London's complex system of postcodes, tactics for booking a table for dinner and what to say when the barman at the local pub calls you "Love". Read on for some quick facts and helpful information when visiting London for the first time.

Ups and downs
Transport

Londoners take this seriously. When you stand on an escalator within the Underground, always stand on the right; you are likely to find someone barking in your ear if you don't. While many British and London traditions are fading – Londoners no longer wait in orderly queues for a bus, for example – the escalator law stands resolute.

Daily greetings
Etiquette

It's a bit of a free for all. Handshakes are likely, kisses (one on each cheek) possible among friends – even work colleagues – but hugs are less common and are not recommended on first introductions. Salutations are equally diverse. You might be greeted with a matronly "Love" or "Darling" by a shopkeeper or barman (perhaps not very PC but who cares – it's authentic). And all sorts of folk will bandy about "Mate" or "Sir" no matter whether they are younger or older than the person being addressed.

One does wish one's corgis were as polite as you are

Postcode lottery
Addresses

Ask 99 per cent of Londoners to explain why an area is SW1 or NW12 and they will soon get flummoxed. The first bit seems easy: SW is for southwest, NW for northwest. But then why do we have an N but no S set of postcodes? And the numbers seem to have been handed out totally illogically; even when you see them on a map they make no sense. OK, this is how it came to be. The Post Office gave the number 1 to the area surrounding its main office in each part of the city then assigned the next numbers according to where sorting offices were located within said district – alphabetically. Let us help with an example. So E1 is where the head office is in the East, E2 is Bethnal Green, E10 Leyton, E17 Walthamstow, etc. In essence it's a system for post workers, not Londoners (let alone visitors). And the reason there is no S is just because someone decided to split it into SW and SE. Their reasoning is best left alone.

Compass connections
Districts

South Londoners and west Londoners support different football teams, have different accents and like different things. And many of them often don't travel far from their "manor". Not because they are scared to, more because they like where they are. But this is not just something that impacts on Londoners who have been here for generations: even new arrivals get caught up in

This is one way to beat congestion

compass-point pride and soon define themselves by where they live (they even get a certain look). The hipsters of east London, for example, would look like exotic birds escaped from London Zoo if they popped up in prim Hampstead. And for some Londoners, crossing the river is best avoided: north Londoners are especially snobby about going south of the Thames. They worry they will need a passport and jabs.

Table manners
Dining

London's top restaurants are often the least helpful. If you actually get through to a real person on the phone and ask for a table for two at 20.00, they may offer you something at 17.30 or 23.00; London's restaurants also struggle to accommodate groups of more than six. Persist. Be nice. Don't beg. Good tables are available if they like the sound of you.

Glass half empty
Drinking

If you get taken to a business lunch it's quite common for people to drink moderately. This is not Utah. Don't be too puritan; go with the flow. Londoners still love a pub

although not as much as they once did. They also love a private members' club – you won't have to make too many acquaintances before you find someone who knows someone, or is indeed the someone you need to know to get in most places.

What's all that digging?
Construction

There are holes all across the city and machines are tunnelling away under your feet. That's because the city is re-engineering how we will get around – and across – London. Crossrail is a new west-east link that involves 21km of new tunnels, 10 new stations and a lot of mud. It's the biggest construction project in Europe and it won't be finished until 2018.

The eastern shift
Gentrification

London may look like an immovable beast but the centre of gravity for the worlds of art, design and having fun have shifted greatly over the past two decades. The rolling waves of hipness and gentrification have enveloped the east of the city. Clerkenwell went first as loft developers moved in during the 1980s, then it was Hoxton and Spitalfields in the 1990s, then Brick Lane and Whitechapel and Dalston. And now you won't find anywhere out east without a great coffee bar run by bearded gents. It's left west London's cooler spots – Notting Hill, for example – to appear, well, not so cool.

Not all rosy
Property

We're sorry to bring this up in a celebratory guide book but you should know that there are some real tensions in the city because of the way that absent overseas buyers have snapped up large chunks of residential London. It means apartments are being used as a means of stashing cash away and it has left some of the swankiest neighbourhoods looking rather sad; you'll notice, for example, that lots of homes in Belgravia remain dark for months on end.

London's favourite tree
Wildlife

London, like many cities, has a tree that it cherishes perhaps above all others. Its leafy canopy and breezy rustle brings to mind summers lolling in the park. It's called the London plane (or, to give it its official name, *Platanus x acerifolia*) and it probably has its roots, so to speak, in varieties from the Orient and Spain but has been popular in the city for several centuries. It flourishes despite the pollution and can even face being stuck in the middle of pavements.

I wonder if this look will work in the artsy East End

Hotels
—— At home in
the capital

London has its share of
storied old hotels and
grand openings but our
fillet of the capital's finest
narrows its gaze and
focuses squarely on hos-
pitality and charm rather
than brand might; good
design rather than bluff
and bluster.

Our smart selection
includes new openings that
are reviving the once-staid
– and hardly stayed-at
– East End hotel scene,
brands well and truly
on the up and a few old
dames taking the best from
their own histories into a
forward-looking present.

From a cosy, curio-
crammed townhouse
conversion to a pied
à terre in well-heeled
Mayfair, each hotel we
have picked out knows
the importance of a pas-
sionate porter, an unflap-
pable GM and, naturally,
a genial barman.

So in that spirit, allow
us to take your coat
and suitcase and whisk
you off on a tour of our
favourite places to rest
our heads.

①
Ham Yard Hotel, Soho
Bountiful boutique

With a portfolio that includes
New York's Crosby Street Hotel
and London's Charlotte Street
premises, Ham Yard is the latest
opening from Tim and Kit Kemp,
the ambitious duo behind the ever-
popular Firmdale Hotels group.

A village-like oasis in the
heart of London's bustling Soho,
the hotel wraps around a green
courtyard, a large-scale bronze
sculpture by Turner Prize-winning
artist Tony Cragg and a cluster of
hand-picked independent shops
that line the hotel's entrance.

Despite its scale, no single
bedroom or suite in the 91-room
hotel feels the same. From the
bespoke wallpaper patterns to the
colourful textiles that upholster
furniture throughout the private
and public spaces, Kit has lovingly
designed every last detail. With
no shortage of entertainment, this
busy establishment also includes
a gym equipped for altitude
training, spa, 190-seat cinema and
restaurant and bar showcasing
the best of British produce. There
is also a fully functioning (and
perhaps somewhat unexpected)
solid-maple bowling alley.
1 Ham Yard, W1D 7DT
+44 (0)20 3642 2000
firmdalehotels.com

MONOCLE COMMENT: The hotel's
event space is bookable seven
days a week and has a dance
floor, lounge and bar. It makes a
great venue to hire, whether for a
private party or an all-important
business bash.

That extra yard
——
Bombed during the Blitz, the
site of the Ham Yard Hotel lay
fallow before being snapped
up by Firmdale in 2009.
Together with architecture
company Woods Bagot, the
firm added large oak trees that
make the Soho passageway
entrance seem like it's been
there for decades.

The Orange, Pimlico
Keeping things simple

Opened in 2009, the Orange Public House and Hotel in residential Pimlico is a half-hour stroll from Tate Britain art gallery and a short dash to preppy Sloane Square for shopping. Run by ex-property developers Barry Hirst and Stefan Turnbull, the homely haunt is filled with wooden details, rustic iron chandeliers and marble fireplaces. Together they convey an eccentric-but-British feel that is more akin to a country cottage than the theatre that once occupied the space.

A narrow staircase leads to the hotel's four rooms that have been designed by leaseholder Cubitt House Group in collaboration with London-based Coote & Bernardi. Expect whites, creamy hues and grey-and-brown furnishings coupled with exposed wooden beams. The marble ensuites are decked out with Aesop bath and beauty products.

After a good night's sleep, a hearty breakfast should follow. The hotel's Severn & Wye smoked-salmon bagel or one of the chef's three-egg omelettes will set you up for the day.

37 Pimlico Road, SW1W 8NE
+44 (0)20 7881 9844
theorange.co.uk

② The Rookery, Clerkenwell
Traditional hospitality and charm

Clerkenwell is no longer the run-down neighbourhood that gave this hotel its name but The Rookery makes every effort to maintain its 18th-century élan. Before it was bought more than 20 years ago by Georgian-architecture aficionados Peter McKay and Douglas Blain, the building was a bacon smokehouse. It was restored, reclad and filled with period furniture, fabrics and tapestries.

Entering the hotel feels like stumbling into a traditional gentleman's club: guests can fix themselves a drink from the bar in the conservatory before reclining on the antique armchairs in front of an open fire. Made up of three listed Georgian houses connected by a succession of velvety corridors, the hotel has 33 rooms, each named after one of the area's former residents – some of them well-to-do and others of less favourable repute.

12 Peter's Lane (off Cowcross Street), EC1M 6DS
+44 (0)20 7336 0931
rookeryhotel.com

MONOCLE COMMENT: Perfect for a romantic tryst, the Rook's Nest is an ornate two-level baroque penthouse with views over the chimney tops to St Paul's Cathedral.

MONOCLE COMMENT: Plump for the Pimlico superior room: it is the largest of the four with plentiful windows for natural light. End the evening with a nightcap of house cocktail Basil Fawlty: Grey Goose vodka, apple juice, passion fruit and homemade basil syrup.

Ⓐ
Claridge's, Mayfair
Art deco delight

A short shopping-bag-laden walk from Bond Street brings you to this redbrick gem known for its plush interior and top-drawer service, nestled in the heart of well-heeled Mayfair. Inside the art deco building you'll find the chessboard-style black-and-white marble floors and crystal chandeliers that have greeted visitors since 1856. Straight ahead is the palatial Foyer restaurant, which serves afternoon tea from the hotel's distinctive gold-rimmed, white-and-jade striped china; to your right is chef Simon Rogan's Michelin-starred Fera restaurant. Oswald Milne's interior dates from the 1920s but has since been updated by designers including Diane von Furstenberg, Guy Oliver and David Linley.

If you're here to stay then the dapper lift operators will guide your ascent to the 197 unique rooms and suites that fill the seven-storey building. The long list of notable guests who have made the same journey include Queen Victoria, Winston Churchill and Audrey Hepburn.
49 Brook Street, W1K 4HR
+44 (0)20 7629 8860
claridges.co.uk

MONOCLE COMMENT: The reputation that Claridge's has for personal service is the envy of hotels worldwide. Facilities may not be the most forward-looking design-wise but no whim is too great or small for the 400-strong team of attentive staff. Old-school comfort is a treat.

Ⓔ
Durrants Hotel, Marylebone
Peace and tranquility

Once a pretty but unremarkable row of townhouses on George Street in London's West End, Durrants Hotel was converted into a 92-room guesthouse back in 1790. It has been in the hands of the Miller family since 1921 and its third-generation owners have worked hard to preserve a country-house feel just steps from the must-shop stop of Marylebone High Street. Oxford Street and the Wallace Collection are also just a few minutes away by foot.

Food comes courtesy of chef Cara Baird and, after an extensive refit in the early 2000s, the hotel is a favourite for functions and business meetings, while private diners can head to the wood-panelled Grill Room restaurant. Pastries and tea are served throughout the day in the Spy Lounge; it is adorned with a collection of caricatures by Sir Leslie Ward, who drew for *Vanity Fair* between the 1870s and early 20th century.
26-32 George Street, W1H 5BJ
+44 (0)20 7935 8131
durrantshotel.co.uk

MONOCLE COMMENT: The private Oak Room can host 24 guests for a business lunch or family gathering.

(6)
Rosewood London, Holborn
Old-school elegance updated

Originally designed to accommodate the carriages that would have pulled up outside when the building was completed in 1914, the elegant Edwardian courtyard of the Rosewood London is a fittingly grand introduction to this High Holborn hotel. Inside, porters dressed in tweed uniforms from British fashion designer Nicholas Oakwell clip across the marble-floored foyer, their footsteps clicking to the chirp of budgies and lovebirds in gilded cages at the hotel's reception.

A seven-storey marble staircase leads up to 44 suites and 262 rooms, each individually furnished and sealed behind hefty Cuban-mahogany doors. Three bar-cum-restaurants suit any occasion. The Holborn Dining Room and Delicatessen is a worthwhile lunching spot that serves a mean charcuterie and scrummy shrimp burger; there's the Mirror Room for afternoon tea or Scarfes Bar for jazz. We'd recommend a Bubble and Shrubs cocktail from Scarfes, made with elderflower, gin and orange bitters. The hotel opened in 2013 and is the first European outpost of the Dallas-based Rosewood Hotels and Resorts group.
252 High Holborn, WC1V 7EN
+ 44 (0)20 7781 8888
rosewoodhotels.com

MONOCLE COMMENT: For a private getaway there's the Manor House Suite and Wing, which has its own entrance, lift and postcode.

Sunday best

Covent Garden Piazza (10 minutes' walk away) was home to London's grocery trade until 1974 but on Sundays the Rosewood's cobbled courtyard hosts a more homely market. Chef Amandine Chaignot's edit of slow-food sellers includes fresh bread and meat and fish, as well as books and blooms.

⑦
The Zetter Townhouse, Clerkenwell
Quirks and cocktails

Tucked behind the unassuming sky-blue door of what could easily be just another London home, The Zetter Townhouse is a breath of fresh air in a world of identikit minimalist hotel design. A taxidermied kangaroo jostles for attention with costumed felines in the hotel's curio-filled lobby, which by night doubles as a cocktail destination favoured by in-the-know locals. It is managed by Tony Conigliaro – a bartender who is to cocktails what René Redzepi is to food – and guests can enjoy creations including the Köln Martini. It is ceremoniously served with a citrus-filled pipette to a background soundtrack of an Édith Piaf *chanson*.

Thanks to former antiques dealer and interior designer Russell Sage, each of the 13 bedrooms in this city bolthole has a personal albeit unorthodox touch. From doors in rooms that double as cheeky windows into bathrooms to hand-knitted hot-water bottles with which guests are provided during the chilly winter months, a sense of craftsmanship pervades the establishment's every design detail.

At mealtimes, guests wanting more than the gourmet snacks served in the lobby bar should take a walk across the cobbled square to the acclaimed Bistrot Bruno Loubet, located in the Townhouse's more modern sister hotel The Zetter.
49-50 St John's Square, EC1V 4JJ
+ 44 (0)20 7324 4550
thezettertownhouse.com

MONOCLE COMMENT: Next door, the Zetter is one of few hotels in the world to boast its own well. Engineers drilled 500 metres below its lobby to source a fresh-water supply that guests at both hotels can sup from bedside bottles.

On the hoof
───

This Regency-style stay is a short walk from the north-eastern tip of Hyde Park and the Serpentine Gallery (*see page 99*). There is a well-trodden path to Oxford Street and the boutiques of Bond Street for savvy shoppers looking for bigger-brand buys.

8

The Grazing Goat, Marylebone
Hidden gem

Waking up to the chiming of church bells is a rare privilege in central London and all the more special if it's achievable within a five-minute walk of bustling Oxford Street. Located on a street in Marylebone that's seconds from the Middle Eastern bustle of Edgware Road, the Grazing Goat has the down-home intimacy of a village inn. Run by Stefan Turnbull and Barry Hirst of The Orange (*see page 17*), the site of the hotel was once a field for the aristocratic Portman family's goats before becoming home to a pub that fell into disrepair.

Now its caramel-coloured panelled walls muffle the sound of the cheerful chatter of punters at the ground-floor bar. In summer, French doors open onto the street but come winter the fireplaces add a comforting glow to proceedings. With only eight rooms available, intimacy is guaranteed. The cosy standard option is roomy enough to host a king-size bed and the sleek marble-and-wood ensuites are stocked with choice cosmetics.

The upstairs dining area with its airy sash windows and cream furniture has a more polished feel than its downstairs counterpart but serves the same simple-yet-refined menu. We'd recommend indulging in the house-cured meats accompanied by sourdough bread and spiced apple-and-tomato chutney.
6 New Quebec Street, W1H 7RQ
+44 (0)20 7724 7243
thegrazinggoat.co.uk

MONOCLE COMMENT: Before heading out to explore the neighbourhood opt for an off-the-menu rosehip negroni, which promises a British twist on the classic apéritif.

Goats
don't
graze
on owls,
correct?

Hotels for people-watching

01 The Berkeley, Knightsbridge: The David Collins-designed Blue Bar (on the left as you enter the hotel) is a favourite for a cocktail with the Knightsbridge evening set. Head barman Stefano Zampieri's mixes are legendary nightcaps. *the-berkeley.co.uk*

02 Soho Hotel, Soho: For those deal-sealing lunches, the film, theatre and music moguls that still work in busy Soho opt for the comfy Refuel restaurant that's part of this Firmdale favourite. *firmdalehotels.com*

03 The Ritz, Piccadilly: Skip the hotel's famous afternoon tea and join the jetsetters within the camphor-wood environs of the Ritz's intimate art deco Rivoli bar. *theritzlondon.com*

04 Park Lane Hotel, Mayfair: Keep an eye out for Park Lane's deep-pocketed Middle Eastern diaspora who make the glitzy strip their base for year-round sprees. Expect plenty of shopping bags and the odd gold-rimmed ride purring outside. *fourseasons.com*

05 Ace Hotel, Shoreditch: From mid-morning on weekdays, entrepreneurs, hipsters and trainer-clad freelancers decamp to this sleek lobby (*see page 27*). They meet, brainstorm, fire off a few emails then celebrate with Kernel craft beers and cocktails come 17.00. *acehotel.com*

Deco style
Best for artful elegance with an edge

(9)

The Beaumont, Mayfair
Classic meets modern

Jeremy King and Chris Corbin are the restaurateurs behind some of London's most acclaimed dining establishments of the past three decades, including The Ivy and Le Caprice. The Beaumont, however, is the duo's first attempt to turn their dab hospitality hand to the hotel trade. Located in a heritage-protected former garage, the 73-room hotel in the heart of Mayfair takes its design cues from the 1920s when it was erected.

Despite its classic art deco-style interior the hotel has become a talking point for the robot-like sculpture that juts out of its stuccoed front. The piece was designed by British artist Antony Gormley and houses an unusual work called "Room": a dark, oak-clad, 10-metre-high suite that guests can stay in.

The hotel's more traditional offerings include a basement spa. The Colony Grill Room and American Bar are failsafe meal-and-cocktail destinations that invoke the atmosphere of the roaring '20s along with a menu offering gourmet executions of comfort-food classics, including a mean macaroni cheese.

*8 Balderton Street, Brown Hart
Gardens, W1K 6TF
+44 (0)20 7499 1001
thebeaumont.com*

MONOCLE COMMENT: For a spot of privacy head to residents' lounge bar The Cub Room.

Will there be
cats to chase
in London?

Dress to impress

The Duke Street area around The Beaumont is a thriving menswear hub. The neighbourhood's tailored offering includes Savile Row tailor Patrick Grant's E Tautz (*see page 50*) for suits or outerwear and Private White VC's shop (*see page 49*).

(10)

Town Hall Hotel, Bethnal Green
Grand transformation

Despite its creative credentials and heady bar scene, east London yields few options for those looking for a plump pillow and a good night's sleep. An exception is the ornate Town Hall Hotel in Bethnal Green, built in 1910 and later extended in art deco style. It's now a welcome addition to the area's gradually improving offerings.

Opened in its current capacity in 2010, the 98-room hotel offers a few carefully preserved clues to the building's municipal past. The one-time council chamber has been transformed into a meeting room replete with leather chairs and fold-down wooden desks, while the Typing Room (also named after its previous purpose) is an inviting restaurant that serves a sumptuous five or seven-course tasting menu.

Upstairs there is another nod to Bethnal Green's past. Sculptures and installations sit alongside marquetry (a technique of inlaying images into wood) by artist Debbie Lawson chronicling Bethnal Green's risqué history.
Patriot Square, E2 9NF
+ 44 (0)20 7871 0460
townhallhotel.com

MONOCLE COMMENT: The popular Peg & Patriot bar is downstairs. Order a Barley & Me cocktail made with burnt-pineapple rum, coconut water, banana-butter syrup, barley wine and lime.

Eastern promise
———
From street level this heritage-protected building doesn't immediately reveal the extension by renovator Rare Architecture. The pattern of the aluminium veil that adorns the wing and roof addition is opaque enough to ensure privacy while also allowing natural light in.

(11)

The Connaught, Mayfair
High-end luxury

Dating from 1897, this grand dame of an establishment is more like a stately home than a traditional hotel. With Wedgwood china and old-fashioned service (each butler is trained to shine shoes at John Lobb and tend to suits at Savile Row tailor Kilgour) it is the anything-but-understated Britishness of proceedings that creates the hotel's charm; think antiques and imperial grandeur with a few stay-making mod cons.

Following a £70m makeover the hotel reopened in 2007 with additional rooms (making 121 in total). There is also an Aman spa with chlorine-free pool, gym and The Apartment: a gargantuan suite with two landscaped terraces that was designed by the late David Collins.

Guests seeking a sense of occasion or dining à deux should head to the hotel's two-Michelin-starred Hélène Darroze restaurant. For pre- or post-prandial cocktails visit the two spectacular bars. There is the Collins-designed Connaught bar, where a signature martini trolley is manned by white-gloved bar staff, or the award-winning Coburg: a whiskey bar renowned for its extensive selection of the spirit.
Carlos Place, W1K 2AL.
+ 44 (0)20 7499 7070
the-connaught.co.uk

MONOCLE COMMENT: The centrepiece of The Connaught is a five-storey solid mahogany Edwardian staircase that is located in front of a lobby desk manned by staff in Nicholas Kirkwood uniforms. Ralph Lauren supposedly fell in love with the stairway on his first visit to the hotel and tried to purchase and export the piece to the US. When his offer was refused, Lauren recreated it in his Madison Avenue flagship store.

Ah, themed relaxation. I call this 'Bubbles'

12

Ace Hotel, Shoreditch
Creative minds

Not content with transforming a
buttoned-down tourist hotel into
Shoreditch's coolest stopover, the
team that brought the Ace Hotel
franchise based in Portland, Oregon,
across the pond has pulled together
a roster of vibrant retailers on its
ground floor. As you enter you will
see coffee from Bulldog Edition,
a collaboration with Square Mile
Coffee Roasters alongside clothing
from New York-based Opening
Ceremony and bouquets from That
Flower Shop, all testament to east
London's blossoming revival.

The impeccably styled rooms
are filled with record players, edgy
murals and bespoke toiletries.
Downstairs, retro-tinged brasserie
Hoi Polloi serves hearty all-day
fare and doubles as a performance
space (think cabaret, artsy rock and
spoken word) while the Miranda bar
is also a late-night must. The seventh
floor offers a gym and sauna as well
as meeting rooms and party spaces
with striking views of the city.

Style in spades
—
Ace may be American but its
first overseas property draws
from a well of London design
talent. Edward Barber and Jay
Osgerby-founded Universal
Design Studio oversaw the
refit, while coin trays come
from British leatherware
specialist Ally Capellino.

With service and substance to
match its on-trend aesthetic, the
Ace Hotel is a one-off in its capacity
to seamlessly bring together suits
and scenesters.
*100 Shoreditch High Street,
E1 6JQ*
+44 (0)20 7613 9800
acehotel.com/london

MONOCLE COMMENT: Cool clientele
and aside, the Ace Hotel's location
is its greatest asset. It sits around
the corner from the boutiques and
bistros of Redchurch Street and
minutes from Brick Lane.

Food and drink
—— The art of dining

London's magnetic pull has tempted some of the world's most promising chefs and restaurateurs to the British capital. But it's not the high-profile crowd-pullers or big-brand openings that fill our culinary hitlist. Instead we have hand-picked the best independent and unique venues for different occasions: from client dinners to must-impress lunches and cosy crannies for dinner à deux. For an added treat we've included an idiosyncratic Indian venue, Polish fare with flair and a Greek restaurant that the locals would rather we kept quiet about.

The vogueish global obsession with filament bulbs and exposed brick walls may be well accounted for in London but it's the variety of utterly unique restaurants and passionate purveyors that show the city in its best light.

Restaurants
Where to eat

①
Rochelle Canteen, Shoreditch
New-school hideaway

Rochelle Canteen served simple lunches to Shoreditch creatives long before it was considered hip to do so. The little sister of Soho watering hole The French House and neighbour to the offices of Frieze – the talented souls behind the magazine and art fair of the same name – the canteen started as a catering firm in 1995. In 2007 its glass concertina doors opened for daytime service.

Located in a converted Victorian school close to a pioneering social-housing project from 1896 – London's first – the canteen features a secluded courtyard that offers a laidback retreat from the East End buzz. The menu changes daily as the chefs favour market-fresh ingredients and experiment with new recipes, all simply executed with French elegance.
Rochelle School, Arnold Circus (just off Club Row), E2 7ES
+44 (0)20 7729 5677
arnoldandhenderson.com

②
Riding House Café, Fitzrovia
Best for brunch

Fitzrovia hasn't always been blessed with destination restaurants so eyebrows were raised when Riding House Café opened in 2011 in a converted 1950s office block. But the diner became a hit with locals for its varied offerings, from brunch to cocktails (it's open until midnight on Fridays and Saturdays). The menu is modern brasserie, heavy on steaks and with an extensive small-plate offering. An added pleasure is spotting BBC execs from nearby New Broadcasting House schmoozing the talent.
43-51 Great Titchfield Street,
W1W 7PQ
+44 (0)20 7927 0840
ridinghousecafe.co.uk

Feeling fresh

Fish is sourced from Devon and Cornwall

London classics

01 Le Caprice, Piccadilly: Richard Caring bought this old gem in 2005 along with its sister The Ivy (see below) and overnight became the king of London's established dining scene. This is white tablecloth and gleaming wine glass territory but oddly cosy, serving timeless dishes from Europe and the US.
le-caprice.co.uk

02 The Ivy, Covent Garden: In its heyday this was the most difficult table in town to secure but recently the Ivy's iconic diamond mullioned windows have seemed a little less opaque and booking has become a less laughable affair. It's still a great place for a stately steak tartare.
the-ivy.co.uk

03 Scott's, Mayfair: A seafood restaurant with an elegant olde-worlde charm. Irish head chef Dave McCarthy serves impeccable shellfish. The mouthwatering selection of oysters is best eaten under the famous black awning outside, weather permitting.
scotts-restaurant.com

04 Wiltons, Piccadilly: After a humble start as an oyster stall in 1742, Wiltons has grown up to become part of the establishment, known and favoured by aristocracy and Whitehall mandarins alike.
wiltons.co.uk

05 Oslo Court, St John's Wood: Oslo Court is like a journey back in time with a menu to match. Expect steak Diane, veal schnitzel Holstein and crab à La Rochelle.
oslocourtrestaurant.co.uk

③
Prawn on the Lawn, Islington
Super seafood

Perched at the rear of St Paul's Road is the splendidly named Prawn on the Lawn. This humble restaurant is an unfussy affair that operates as a fishmonger by day before pulling out a few seats and firing up the hob by night. The fish is as fresh as it gets (in landlocked London at least), delivered daily from the UK's southwest coast. Scallop ceviche, monkfish-and-chorizo stew and split langoustine are some of the highlights of the ever-changing menu – paired with homemade soda bread and a manzanilla sherry, of course.
220 St Paul's Road, N1 2LL
+44 (0)20 3302 8668
prawnonthelawn.com

④
Dinings, Marylebone
Cosy Japanese

Fresh European produce and well-honed Japanese dishes make this unassuming Edwardian townhouse an unmissable destination for an intimate dinner. It was founded in 2006 by former Nobu colleagues Tomonari Chiba, Keiji Fuku, Masaki Sugisaki and Nick Taylor-Guy and getting a table can be an issue at the 28-seat stop. If you're lucky enough to grab a perch on the benches, the Tar-Tar chips – crisp potato creations served with a choice of vegetable, fish or meat fillings – are an apt introduction to its sophisticated tapas-style dishes.
22 Harcourt Street, W1H 4HH
+ 44 (0)20 7723 0666
dinings.co.uk

⑤
Khan's, Notting Hill
An Indian fantasia

Gone are the hedonistic nights of this west London fixture – once beloved of expense-account entertainers hollering for endless trays of cheap pints and big curries – but all is not lost. The trompe l'oeil walls are all Raj perfection (as painted by numbers by a nine-year-old), the palm-tree pillars have been regilded and the butter chicken remains the best in London. It will have to be washed down by a mocktail rather than a cheap lager now the joint no longer serves alcohol but the expertly spiced curry is still great value.
13-15 Westbourne Grove, W2 4UA
+ 44 (0)20 7727 5420
khansrestaurant.com

Curry cravings

Since London's first Indian restaurant opened in 1810, the Brits have been curry mad. So much so that many people view chicken tikka masala (with pilau rice and a soft naan, of course) as Britain's rightful national dish.

⑥
Koya, Soho
Udon utopia

This Japanese *udonya* run by head chef Junya Yamasaki has made a splash with a repertoire that goes beyond its springy signature ingredient. Yamasaki uses British produce to compile an innovative Japanese menu. Choose from the specials: they change daily, chalked up on the blackboard where Yamasaki's team presents seasonal dishes. Expect wild-rabbit confit with carrot, red turnip and broad-bean salad; there's also skate-wing-and-cucumber-leaf tempura or stout-and-honey-braised pork belly.
49 Frith Street, W1D 4SG
+44 (0)20 7434 4463
koya.co.uk

Chocolate shops

01 Paul A Young, citywide: Award-winning British chocolatier Young and his team make the city's finest sea-salt caramel-filled chocolate.
paulayoung.co.uk

02 Rococo, citywide: Chantal Coady's shop is an artistically put-together space. Try the delicious house truffles.
rococochocolates.com

03 Mast Brothers, Shoreditch: This Brooklyn chocolatier has the first commercial bean-to-bar chocolate factory in London plus a café and a shop. Chocolate bars are all made on the spot.
mastbrothers.com

❼
La Famiglia, Chelsea
Leisurely lunch

Opened in 1966 by the late Alvaro Maccioni, this family-run institution in southwest London's well-heeled Chelsea is still going strong. Located on a quiet street off the King's Road, La Famiglia has a top-notch menu of Tuscan-influenced delights. Food-wise it's a no-tricks, few-frills kind of place but that's what you want from an Italian: great quality and an atmosphere to boot. It's a good spot for lunch but comes alive at night, especially when the patio is opened to diners during the summer.
7 Langton Street, The World's End, SW10 0JL
+44 (0)20 7351 0761
lafamiglia.co.uk

8
The Palomar, Piccadilly
Friendly service

Run by the team behind Jerusalem's
hip Machneyuda restaurant and
two siblings who owned iconic
London nightclub The End,
The Palomar is a mixture of
Mediterranean, Arabic and Jewish
cuisine brought together in a playful
atmosphere. Devotees flock for
dishes from the raw bar including
kubenia – hand-chopped beef
fillet with bulgur, tahini, pine nuts
and herbs – which pairs well with
buttery *kubaneh* (Yemeni bread)
and tomato sauce. From the hot
kitchen there is sirloin steak with
latkes (potato pancakes) and a
mustard-cream coriander sauce.
    Be sure to book ahead. For walk-
ins the leather bar seats operate on
a first-come, first-served basis. Be
warned: diners in this privileged
perch have been spotted knocking
back digestifs with the chefs on the
opposite side of the counter.
34 Rupert Street, W1D 6DN
+44 (0)20 7439 8777
thepalomar.co.uk

Bonnie Gull
SEAFOOD SHACK

Today's Catch

9
Bonnie Gull Seafood Shack,
Fitzrovia
Sea change

Fish and chips may not have the
culinary cachet of other more
sophisticated national dishes but
the beer-battered North Sea
haddock with dripping chips
and mushy peas at the Bonnie
Gull Seafood Shack could well
convince the doubters. What
started in Islington as a temporary
restaurant run by co-founder
Alex Hunter and Danny Clancy
has blossomed into one of our
favourite Fitzrovia stop-ins since
opening in early 2013.
    Look past the seaside kitch for
the chalkboard map of the UK that
charts the daily haul of fresh
seafood on offer, plus the artfully
arranged cold bar showcasing
oysters. The Bonnie Gull's second
venue opened its porthole in
Exmouth Market in 2014.
21A Foley Street, W1W 6DS
+44 (0)20 7436 0921
bonniegull.com

(11)
Ibérica, Farringdon
Sublime Spanish cuisine

If you don't fancy a 05.00 rise for a glimpse of the impressive Smithfield meat market nearby, book a table at Ibérica to sample some of the tastiest examples of what these cuts can become. Located in Farringdon, the Spanish restaurant is perfect for sharing platters of *jamón ibérico* (cured for at least 45 months) and mini burgers stuffed with tender pork loin and *piparra* peppers. Take a perch on the high leather stools in front of the ornate gold detailing of the bar for a taste of the menu concocted by two-Michelin-starred chef Nacho Manzano.
89 Turnmill Street, EC1M 5QU
+44 (0)20 7636 8650
ibericarestaurants.com

I'll probably have that first Michelin star by the time this is cooked

10
St John, Farringdon
Private-dining delight

Twenty years on from its launch, Fergus Henderson's nose-to-tail eating revolution still influences chefs, menus and working practices across the UK and over the pond. The menu is a thing of simple beauty: no tautology, just produce. St John's anti-decorative aesthetic has been aped everywhere, too; even chain diners are now done out like ersatz butcher's shops. You will always eat wonderfully at St John, even if you confine yourself to roots and fruits. Henderson knows meat is precious so expect small, honed dishes.
26 St John Street, EC1M 4AY
+44 (0)20 7251 0848
stjohngroup.uk.com

Out of office
Small dishes are perfect for a working lunch

Get a room

Special occasion? St John's plush private dining room is an intimate 16-seat affair in the building's former loading bay. Alternatively, for a bigger bash you can rent the whole Spitalfields restaurant in east London, which seats 60.

Bakeries

01 St John Bakery, Bermondsey: Rising to the lofty benchmark set by his restaurants (*see previous page*), Fergus Henderson's bakery is at its best (and busiest) on Saturdays when doughnuts or hot-from-the-oven madeleines draw the crowds.
stjohngroup.uk.com/bakery

02 Balthazar Boulangerie, Covent Garden: Chef Keith McNally's New York mainstay opened its London branch to some fanfare in Covent Garden in 2013. Despite all the noise of the launch, the space has settled into a quiet favourite for lovers of filo tarts, croissants and cinnamon swirls.
balthazarlondon.com/boulangerie

03 Brick House, Peckham Rye: The understated oven junkies of Brick House are flying the flag for real bread in London's often overlooked southeast. The Peckham Rye loaf is one of the main draws at the specialist sourdough bakers located close to Peckham Rye Common.
brickhousebread.com

⑫ Donostia, Marylebone
Basque in the limelight

Spanish restaurants are abundant in London; Basque specialists less so. Luckily, Donostia's delicious interpretation of the regional cuisine makes up for its lack of sparring partners. The spare decor might disguise its Iberian roots but the *jamón* hanging in the window points to its origins. "We don't do any of those tourist-destination dishes," says co-owner Nemanja Borjanovic. Instead, Polish head chef Damian Surowiec delivers pitch-perfect regional delicacies including Basque steak or crisp cod cheeks with tangy squid-ink aioli.
*10 Seymour Place, W1H 7ND
+44 (0)20 3620 1845
donostia.co.uk*

(13)
Lemonia, Primrose Hill
Best-kept secret

Gems like this Greek taverna are hard to find: always busy and run by penguined-up older waiters who carry out their duties with a healthy dose of wit and a wry smile. The food at Lemonia is homely and satisfying and the service (although brisk by some tastes) is never rude. Go for the houmous and tzatziki to start, plus calamari and the artichoke and broad beans; then plump for the slow-cooked lamb *kleftiko* or moussaka for main. The Turkish delight they dish out with the surprisingly reasonable bill is second to none.

89 Regent's Park Road, NW1 8UY
+ 44 (0)20 7586 7454
lemonia.co.uk

You'd better not be thinking of serving me up on a platter

Breakfast spots

01 **Nopi, Soho:** Named for its location (north of Piccadilly), Nopi is the sophisticated brother in the Ottolenghi restaurant family. Our pick of the breakfast menu? *Shakshuka*: a mix of braised eggs, piquante tomato sauce and smoked *labneh* (yoghurt). *nopi-restaurant.com*

02 **The Wolseley, Piccadilly:** This former car salesroom was converted into a Mitteleuropa-style café in 2003 with a grand decor that makes it feel centuries old. The eggs Benedict is a classic but don't let the highfalutin reputation throw you: this is the place for a business breakfast with someone you like. *thewolseley.com*

03 **Granger & Co, Clerkenwell:** Aussie-born chef Bill Granger burst onto the London scene serving hearty brunches with Antipodean ease. Both his scrambled eggs and ricotta hotcakes are near-legendary. *grangerandco.com*

04 **Cecconi's, Mayfair:** The breakfast is reliable (some may say unadventurous) but it is the setting and stylish metropolitan crowd that makes people come – and come back. *cecconis.co.uk*

05 **Albion, Shoreditch:** Sir Terence Conran's modern take on London's "greasy spoon" cafés, the Albion is heavy on British produce. Located on the ground floor of the Boundary Hotel, it has an open bakery and kitchen that add an alluring aroma to proceedings. *albioncaff.co.uk*

Feeling indecisive?

Leave the difficult choices to the professionals and order from the set menu. You'll receive a tasty selection of punchy, seasonal mezze followed by your choice of a main and something sweet to round things off.

⑭

Honey & Co, Fitzrovia
Middle Eastern marvel

Pastries rolled with fig or sprinkled with pistachios entice passers-by at this masterful purveyor of Middle Eastern cuisine, while colourful jars of preserves attest to the region's natural pantry. The menu offers the kind of comfort food husband-and-wife co-founders (and chefs) Itamar Srulovich and Sarit Packer remember from their Israeli childhoods and the white-and-blue tiled dining room buzzes from breakfast to dinner. "There's a lot of goodwill for restaurants and quality food in this town," says Srulovich.
25A Warren Street, W1T 5LZ
+44 (0)20 7388 6175
honeyandco.co.uk

15
Hix, Soho
Post-theatre dining

Instead of being sucked into one of
the West End's crowded, neon-lit
dining rooms after the theatre,
make tracks for the heavy wooden
door of chef Mark Hix's Brewer
Street outpost. The second-born
of his seven London venues has
a set menu available well after the
curtain drops. Expect rethought
British specialities, including
succulent veal sausage and a
rich Bakewell tart. Barman Nick
Strangeway conjures experimental
cocktails downstairs; it's up to you
whether they serve as a nightcap or
the opening act of an evening out.
66-70 Brewer Street, W1F 9UP
+44 (0)20 7292 3518
hixsoho.co.uk

Must-try
Bagel from Beigel Bake,
Shoreditch
Although the street is known
for its ubiquitous curry houses
– few worth sampling, many
worth actively avoiding – and
vintage-clothes hunters,
it's the bagels that keep us
wending our way to Brick
Lane. Beigel Bake is a 24-hour
bakery that has kept passing
revellers with rumbling
tummies happy since 1977.
The salmon-and-cream-
cheese is a favourite but our
pick is a tender salt beef with
mustard and pickle.
beigelbake.com

16
Fischer's, Marylebone
Heart-of-Europe cooking

Although it opened in 2014,
Fischer's has an established,
meant-to-be-here feel to it. The
design is grand and Viennese and
the menu boasts chopped liver and
käsespätzle (Austrian macaroni
and cheese), Wiener schnitzel or
a choice of London's best *wurst*
for mains. It's from the team
behind The Wolseley (*see opposite
page*) and The Delaunay and
feels as much an institution in the
making – but Fischer's succeeds
in achieving a far cosier ambience
than its bigger-name stablemates.
50 Marylebone High Street,
W1U 5HN
+44 (0)20 7466 5501
fischers.co.uk

Tea shops

01 My Cup of Tea, Soho:
There's an apothecary-
like feel to the piled-
high blends and tisanes
available from Ausra
Burg's pretty shop on the
ground floor of the Ham
Yard Hotel (*see page 16*).
mycupoftea.co.uk

02 Fortnum & Mason,
Piccadilly: Fortnum &
Mason's Earl Grey (a
British favourite with
a hint of bergamot) is
unparalleled and one
reason this Grand Dame
of a department store has
survived and thrived for
the past three centuries.
fortnumandmason.com

03 Postcard Teas, Mayfair:
A brew easily enjoyed
in good conscience;
sales of Postcard's
60-strong selection go to
support small farms and
co-operatives around the
world that are all fewer
than 6 hectares in size.
postcardteas.com

*London's
choice of tea
shops is very
refreshing*

Buon appetito
—
Best Italian for a must-impress meeting

⑰
The River Café, Hammersmith
Best for a client dinner

Started in 1987 as a canteen for her architect husband's next-door studio, Ruth Rogers' café is an ever-popular Thames-side restaurant in the southwest suburb of Hammersmith. Despite being self-taught, she won a Michelin star in 1997, which the River Café retains, so booking in advance is advised.

Inside the 120-cover space are colourful and crisp interiors – including an open oven with a bright pink cover – all designed by Ruth's husband (and famed British architect) Richard Rogers. The menu changes daily depending on the produce available but whatever's in stock, the pasta dishes are London's most inventive. For pudding we'd suggest pitting your appetite against the signature Chocolate Nemesis, an indulgently rich dark-chocolate torte.
Thames Wharf, Rainville Road,
W6 9HA
+ 44 (0)20 7386 4200
rivercafe.co.uk

Inventive seasonal Italian cuisine

Patisseries

01 Lanka, Finchley:
Japanese-born pastry chef Masayuki Hara creates light and tasty gourmet cakes flavoured with green tea or *matcha* and the capital's most mouthwatering macarons.
lanka-uk.com

02 Maison Bertaux, Soho:
The best buns and *café au lait* this side of the Channel are served under the blue-and-white striped awning of this institution.
maisonbertaux.com

03 Louis Patisserie, Hampstead: Right in the heart of Hampstead, this tea room-cum-bakery offers an irresistible selection of traditional Hungarian cakes; try the poppy-seed creation.
+44 (0)20 7435 9908

⑱
The Providores, Marylebone
First place for fusion

The Providores has a split-floor personality. Downstairs you'll find yourself sat at a tiny wooden table having a tapas-style experience; upstairs you'll be running your hands across the white table linen and enjoying more traditional dining. But what unites the two floors is the cooking of Kiwi Peter Gordon. Both menus are a torrent of dishes made from worldly ingredients. How about a spiced dahl-stuffed tempura *inari* pocket with aubergine, spinach and yellowbean ginger dressing? You get the idea.
109 Marylebone High Street,
W1U 4RX
+ 44 (0)20 7935 6175
theprovidores.co.uk

A light snack will see me through until teatime

Where you'll find our editors in Marylebone

Monocle Café: For a morning flat white.
Il Blandford's: For an old-school Italian lunch.
Hardy's: For a post-work glass of wine.
Diwan: For Lebanese take-out.
Chiltern Firehouse: For a late-night cocktail.

Must-try
Porterhouse steak from Hawksmoor, Piccadilly
With five restaurants in London and now one in Manchester too, there is clearly an appetite for Hawksmoor's New York-influenced take on tastebud-tingling steaks. Best enjoyed medium rare, the dictionary-thick porterhouse (a fillet and sirloin separated by a T-bone) comes from 30-month-old Longhorn cattle that are reared in North Yorkshire. Sides including creamed spinach and triple-cooked chips ensure that you will leave satisfied.
thehawksmoor.com

(19)
Ciao Bella, Bloomsbury
Hearty Italian portions

Lambs Conduit Street has become the go-to spot for menswear and domestic design but, while fashions change, Ciao Bella just keeps on doing its thing. This simple Italian restaurant (you come here for mighty pizzas and big bowls of pasta) has pleasant staff who have aged with the business; there's also a pianist in the evenings and no pretension. That's why what should be just a neighbourhood joint has become a siren, pulling in lovers of *quattro formaggi* from across London.
86-90 Lambs Conduit Street, WC1N 3LZ
+44 (0)20 7242 4119
ciaobellarestaurant.co.uk

(20)
Daquise, South Kensington
Homely Polish welcome

London is home to a large number of Polish people who headed here after the nation joined the EU. But back in the 1940s this restaurant was at the heart of an earlier community of Poles who fled their homeland first to fight the Nazis and then the Soviets. Indeed, Edward Raczynski, Polish president in exile at the time, used the restaurant as an unofficial HQ. The food, you say? Ah, yes. Daquise has been serving hearty Polish meals all this time so if you hanker after a bit of carp, this is your spot.
20 Thurloe Street, SW7 2LT
+44 (0)20 7589 6117
daquise.co.uk

㉑

Quality Chop House, Farringdon
Meat feast

A short walk from Exmouth
Market brings you to the Quality
Chop House, a traditional-feeling
restaurant dating back to 1869. The
clientele may have changed over
the years but a pleasing Victorian
feel remains. The dining room is
filled with booths and benches
and nightly feasts are served from
shared tables. The menu includes
shoulder of Blackface lamb,
sumptuous chops (of course),
Longhorn beef, rabbit loin and
marrowbone fritters. Dishes are
accompanied by a wonderfully
Catholic wine list.
88-94 Farringdon Road, EC1R 3EA
+44 (0)20 7278 1452
thequalitychophouse.com

Drinks
Bottoms up

①

The Monocle Café, Marylebone
Print and percolators

The Monocle Café opened its doors
on Marylebone's Chiltern Street in
2013, just steps from our nearby HQ
and our shop on George Street. Our
in-house design team transformed
the two-storey space, furnished
with tables and feather-upholstered
sofas where you can make yourself
at home with a cup of Allpress
coffee, pick up the latest issue of
the magazine and bump into fellow
readers. The café's team serves
a range of global cuisine – from
Scandinavian pastries to chicken
udon soup – to the tune of Monocle
24. Meanwhile, the café basement
is available to hire for breakfast
meetings, afternoon pitches and
casual drinks.
18 Chiltern Street, W1U 7QA
+44 (0)20 7135 2040
cafe.monocle.com

Coffee shops

London's once Starbucks-
dominated coffee scene has
enjoyed a renaissance, mainly
due to independent baristas
and coffee enthusiasts from
Australia and the US's West
Coast bringing some well-
pulled espresso to the capital.

01 Workshop, Clerkenwell:
The fourth outpost of the
Aussie beansters is a 25-
seat horseshoe-shaped
bar serving enviable
macchiatos made using
coffee roasted at its
flagship Clerkenwell base.
workshopcoffee.com

02 Kaffeine, Fitzrovia:
Besides the (strong)
brews there is also
a decent selection
of breads, biscuits,
chutneys, jams, muffins
and pies, all made on
site and from scratch.
kaffeine.co.uk

03 The Espresso Room,
Bloomsbury: Donald
Judd-inspired interiors, a
larch-and-concrete palette
and perhaps London's
best flat white, served in
a single room near Lambs
Conduit Street.
theespressoroom.com

04 Allpress, Shoreditch:
New Zealander Michael
Allpress's all-conquering
coffee enjoys a pretty
east London pitch on
Redchurch Street, the
area's main retail stretch.
allpressespresso.com

05 Talkhouse Coffee,
Notting Hill: Offers
gourmet coffee made
in Aeropress machines
with beans sourced from
Workshop and Square
Mile Coffee Roasters. The
accompanying brunch
and lunch options are
simple staples such as
pancakes with blueberries
and maple syrup.
talkhousecoffee.com

② Hardy's, Marylebone
Old-school brasserie

Many of our staff members can attest to the restorative powers of the extensive wine list at Hardy's (full disclosure: our London headquarters are adjacent). The charming French-style brasserie features a 36-seat subterranean Underbar area that is perfect for late-night events. Head chef Sam Hughes's menu veers from fish and chips and shepherd's pie to French delicacies.
53 Dorset Street, W1U 7NH
+44 (0)20 7935 5929
hardysbrasserie.com

Favourite wine bars

01 Antidote, Soho
antidotewinebar.com
02 Sager + Wilde, Hoxton
sagerandwilde.com
03 Dean Street Townhouse, Soho
deanstreettownhouse.com

③ Roots & Bulbs, Marylebone
Refreshing pit-stop

Sarah Cadji's shop sells healthy blends from the city's first standalone cold-pressed juice bar and has been making vegetable-and-fruit creations since early 2014. The lower heat that is used to cook them ensures the blends remain nutrient-rich and delightfully aromatic.
5 Thayer Street, W1U 3JG
+44 (0)20 7488 2900
rootsandbulbs.com

Must-try
Oysters and Guinness from The Cow, Westbourne Park
It's neither in Ireland nor by the sea but you'd never know that based on the Guinness and oysters at this traditional west London gaff. The delicacy is broadcast from a neon sign above the door but on the ground floor the pub is a traditional affair. Upstairs it gives way to a fish-focused restaurant where whelks, winkles and prawns are served to the taste of owner Tom Conran. The Cow is a favourite with locals so reserve your upper-room table in advance if you don't fancy the cosy banquette seating downstairs.
thecowlondon.co.uk

Cocktail bars

01 69 Colebrooke Row, Angel: Barman Tony Conigliaro's snug, film-noir-feeling cocktail spot has set the standard in London since opening in 2009. *69colebrookerow.com*

02 Chiltern Firehouse, Marylebone: Hotelier André Balazs' converted gothic-style fire station features food by Michelin-starred chef Nuno Mendes and a garden terrace. A favourite for client-schmoozing lunches and celebrities in dark glasses, the marble bar is a perfect perch for people-watching. *chilternfirehouse.com*

03 Dukes, Mayfair: A favourite haunt of James Bond creator Ian Fleming, the forest-green chairs of Alessandro Palazzi's bar are the only place to enjoy a martini. Expect white-jacketed waiters and a drink worthy of its on-the-high-side price tag. *dukeshotel.com*

04 Upstairs at Rules, Covent Garden: With clients including royalty and nobility this plush bar above London's oldest restaurant (Rules opened in 1798) is headed by barman Chris Lacey and remains a well-kept secret. *rules.co.uk*

05 Beagle, Hoxton: Head to the railway arches by Hoxton Overground station for a choice of superlative Bloody Marys. Beagle offers four twists on the classic drink including a chorizo-infused vodka or smoked-garlic tequila as a base. *beaglelondon.co.uk*

I like to bring my bespoke pint glass with me of an evening

Pubs

01 **Prince Alfred, Maida Vale:** Carved mahogany snugs with glass detailing and the sky-lit Formosa dining room make this Victorian pub an atmospheric addition to your tour of northwest London.
theprincealfred.com

02 **Lansdowne, Primrose Hill:** The white-tiled exterior and outdoor benches belie the quality of the food and drink on offer in this understated Primrose Hill local.
thelansdownepub.co.uk

03 **Royal Oak, Hoxton:** A favourite with Columbia Road's flower-market admirers, the central bar is bustling at weekends. Ales and lagers come from craft-beer maker Camden Town Brewery.
royaloaklondon.com

04 **Carpenters Arms, Whitechapel:** Once owned by notorious gangster twins Ronnie and Reggie Kray, this bar close to Brick Lane has shed its sinister past and now offers friendly service and a choice of 50 ales.
carpentersarmsfree house.com

05 **Nags Head, Knightsbridge:** Not to be mistaken for the risqué gentleman's venue of the same name, this is a charming curio-crammed villagey affair of wood panelling, low ceilings and English ales.
+44 (0)20 7235 1135

Dogs welcome
—
The Bull & Last provides treats for pet pooches

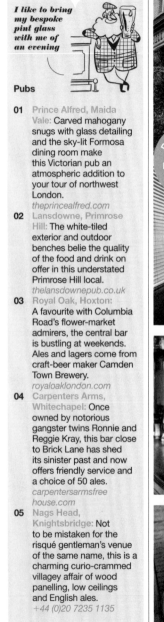

④
The Bull & Last, Hampstead Heath
Lazy Sundays

Located across from the grassy 320-hectare expanse of Hampstead Heath, The Bull & Last pub is the perfect spot for a post-ramble pint or an intimate candle-lit dinner. Regulars at this former 19th-century coaching inn – one of London's finest gastropubs – include food critics, families and north London liberals. Expect a cosy, countrified setting with rustic wooden furniture, taxidermy bulls' heads on the walls and warm fires come winter. The menu is consistently excellent, with an outstanding charcuterie board featuring a notable duck prosciutto.

On weekends expect an elegant take on the British roast with North Essex Shorthorn beef, Yorkshire puddings, roast potatoes, carrots and tangy horseradish sauce. All the ingredients you need for a leisurely Sunday.
168 Highgate Road, NW5 1QS
+44 (0)20 7267 3641
thebullandlast.co.uk

Local flavour
Food markets

London's population will reach
10 million by 2030 but the city
isn't hooked on supermarkets
yet – rather, there's a new sense
of localism in the food industry.
With "small-scale", "ethical"
and "traceable" the watchwords,
markets have become proving
grounds for innovators. While
Smithfield meat market in
Farringdon and Billingsgate fish
market in The City have remained
resolutely wholesale affairs, plenty
of London's markets have found
new leases of life in catering
directly to the city's food-conscious
consumers. Here are three of
our favourites.

① Borough
Home of the food revolution

London's love affair with the
provenance of its food may seem
like a recent infatuation but this
spot, between Southwark Street
and Borough High Street south
of the Thames, has been a hub for
produce since 1756.

The covered market's vibrancy
belies its age and has transformed
from a boisterous business-to-
business affair into a test for
both the capital's new food
entrepreneurs and established
purveyors. More than 100 stalls
touting oven-fresh bread, potted
conserves and traceable meat stir
the senses and vie for attention
with Vietnamese street food, cakes
and delicate confectionery. Your
appetite is your only limitation.
*8 Southwark Street, SE1 1TL.
boroughmarket.org.uk*

THREE STALLS TO STOP AT

01 **Brindisa for Spanish food**
brindisa.com
02 **The Ginger Pig for fresh-
from-the-butcher sausage rolls**
thegingerpig.co.uk
03 **Kappacasein for an
unforgettable melted-cheese-
and-leek sandwich**
kappacasein.com

② Greenwich
Riverside grazing

Home to the Royal Observatory
and National Maritime Museum,
Greenwich is a World Heritage site
and the traditional departure point
for London's once-thriving shipping
trade (which is why Greenwich
Mean Time is measured from here).
It also has a great covered market.

Head past the vintage clothes,
prints and ceramics to the small
businesses reviving the market's
reputation. The best time to visit is
at weekends; you'll still need sharp
elbows but it's a civilised alternative
to the central-London crush.
*5B Greenwich Market, SE10 9HZ
greenwichmarketlondon.com*

THREE STALLS TO STOP AT:

01 Rubys of London for delicate
cupcakes
rubysoflondon.com
02 Arapina's for fresh muffins
arapina.co.uk
03 Brazilian Churros for just that
– with *dulce de leche*, of course
+44 (0)7415 232 191

*Of course, I could
just pop down
to Greenwich
market*

③ Maltby Street
Innovation beneath the arches

Once home to oily garages and
warehouse storage units, the
railway arches of Bermondsey in
southeast London have been
turned into a gourmet's dream.
While the preserved archways add
an industrial feel to the area (case
in point is Lassco architectural
salvage shop), the addition of the
Ropewalk – a stretch of pop-ups
and stalls between Maltby Street
and Millstream Road – and the Spa
Terminus site 10 minutes' walk
away has yielded everything from
urban-farmed honey and English
preserves to Swiss cheese.

For a taste of the inventiveness on
offer try mead, a honey-based brew
that has been revived by brewer
Gosnells. You can also enjoy a
currywurst from Herman Ze
German or a *kielbasa* (smoked
sausage) from Topolski.
*Ropewalk, SE1 2HQ
maltby.st*

THREE STALLS TO STOP AT

01 Neal's Yard Dairy for Cornish
Yarg or a Shropshire Blue
nealsyarddairy.co.uk
02 Monmouth Coffee for a perky
pick-me-up
monmouthcoffee.co.uk
03 Kernel Brewery for a local ale
thekernelbrewery.com

Retail
— A nation of shopkeepers

Concept stores
Smartly mixed retail

Whether it's small-yet-recognisable brand names, a fresh designer making a mark in the capital or old chaps with new-found glory, London knows how to cater to the most exigent of tastes. Of course there are also the big brands and global fast-fashion retailers but we've always had a soft spot for independent outfits. Besides a couple of department stores, most of the ventures in the following pages are small and snug.

There are also a few non-British surprises – NikeLab (one of Europe's best places to buy trainers) and Native & Co (a great choice of Asian designs) – that occupy an important niche. From mixed retail, clothing and accessories to kids' toys, books and record shops, we hope that the following pages will prove handy and inspiring when embarking on your shopping spree in London.

①
Goodhood, Hoxton
Institution of style

With its street-style chutzpah the Goodhood Store in Hoxton, east London, has been a fashion and homeware destination since opening in 2007.

In 2014 the shop moved to a bigger two-storey home on Curtain Road around the corner from its original premises. The brand's co-founder Jo Sindle (*pictured, on left*) says, "We retained elements of the old store but have experimented with new materials including wood, concrete and marble."

Expect menswear and womenswear from Scandinavia, Japan and the US, skincare and grooming products, and children's toys and clothing. There is also pottery by Judy Jackson Stoneware, Ferm Living cushions, Muuto lamps and plenty more to add charm and comfort to your home.
151 Curtain Road, EC2A 3QE
+44 (0)20 7729 3600
goodhoodstore.com

Jo Sindle's favourite shops in London

01 Aram Store: "An inspiring selection of furnishings and interior design near Covent Garden."
aram.co.uk

02 Supreme: "Our favourite stop for casualwear on London's Peter Street."
supremenewyork.com

03 Bottle Apostle: "A little wine shop in Victoria Park selling everything from the nicest affordable bottle to wines for special occasions."
bottleapostle.com

② Trunk Clothiers and Trunk Labs, Marylebone
Impeccable global edit

With two shops on Chiltern Street, Trunk is an integral part of the fabric of this well-turned-out neighbourhood. Trunk Clothiers was established in 2010 with a view to shaking up the capital's menswear offering: the shop houses a range of brands from Japan, Scandinavia, the US, Italy and beyond, chosen with a keen eye for detail by Mats Klingberg. Look out for the latest by the likes of Boglioli, Barena, Mackintosh and Alden.

Just down the road at number 34 is Trunk Labs, an accessories shop for those looking to add a touch of style to their look, office or home. It is the only retailer outside Japan for Ichizawa Shinzaburo Hanpu bags and also stocks luggage by Rimowa and skincare products by Aesop. And full disclosure: the shop is a cousin to MONOCLE.
8 Chiltern Street, W1U 7PU
+ 44 (0)20 7486 2357
trunkclothiers.com

LUGGAGE
ACCESSORIES
BAGS
SHOES

L A B S

③ The Shop at Bluebird, Chelsea
High-concept design

The Shop at Bluebird is a King's Road institution. Filling the space that was once a showroom for Bluebird cars, the Jigsaw-owned concept store has been parading luxury and contemporary design-led labels since 2005 and now has an offshoot: the Duke Street Emporium. "We don't flick in and out of brands season by season, instead we prefer to work with labels for years," says Claire Miles, head of The Shop at Bluebird. His-and-hers fashion, homeware and books span the expanse of this slick store.
350 King's Road, SW3 5UU
+ 44 (0)20 7351 3873
theshopatbluebird.com

TOP PICKS
01   Grooming products from
      London-based Carter
      and Bond
02   Sunglasses from Eye
      Respect London
03   Shoes by Grenson

④

Monocle Shop, Marylebone
Books, magazines and more

Our very own shop on George Street in the heart of Marylebone, central London, is the ideal place to pick up a back issue of the magazine or one of our books published by Gestalten. You can also get your hands on some of the many accessories and clothes we've produced in collaboration with brands such as Begg & Co, Porter, Andersen-Andersen and Oyuna through the years.

You'll also find smaller products designed by our team in London and produced in Europe, such as oak-and-brass paperweights and our signature linen-covered notebooks. The Monocle Shop is just a short hop from the Monocle Café on Chiltern Street and our HQ at Midori House. If you're in the neighbourhood, pop in and say hello.
2A George Street, W1U 3QS
+44 (0)20 7486 8770
monocle.com/shop

⑤

Present London, Shoreditch
Cool Britannia updated

Opened in 2009 in Shoreditch, Present is a mixed-retail concept store from Eddie Prendergast, who as co-founder of clothing label Duffer of St George was instrumental in the Cool Britannia fashion scene of the 1990s. With Present he's added a grown-up edge, bringing us international gems such as Haversack and Hartford, as well as stocking British brands such as William Fox & Sons and Hancock.

Besides its own Present clothing range the retailer has also embarked on a series of collaborations, including brogue boots made with Tricker's and men's tops with Savile Row veteran Hardy Amies. While you're in the neighbourhood, go for a flat white at nearby Ozone Coffee Roasters on Leonard Street.
140 Shoreditch High Street, E1 6JE
+44 (0)20 7033 0500
present-london.com

TOP PICKS
01 'Made in Scotland' cardigans by Present
02 Raincoats by Hancock
03 Blazers by Harris Wharf London
04 Grooming sets by Gentlemen's Tonic
05 Backpacks and leather goods by Daines & Hathaway

Department stores
Everything under one roof

01 Liberty, Mayfair: Set in a Tudor-revival building (sadly the façade dates back to 1924 rather than the 1500s) in the heart of London's luxury district, Liberty is one of the few traditional emporiums of its kind left in the world. It was conceived by Arthur Lasenby Liberty in 1875 as a purveyor of ornaments, fabrics and *objets d'art* from Japan and the Far East. Although best known for its floral-patterned fabrics, its six floors contain everything from popular menswear and womenswear brands to rarer labels, which are all found alongside the Liberty London in-house collections. Even if you're not planning on buying anything it's worth wandering around for a lingering marvel.
liberty.co.uk

02 Peter Jones, Chelsea: With its west London location in chic Sloane Square opposite the Royal Court Theatre, Peter Jones is the most upmarket member of the John Lewis group of department stores and an ideal destination if you're searching for gifts or life's essentials to take back with you. Look out for candles and fragrances by True Grace and Jo Malone and homeware by Alessi, among others. On the fashion side you'll find high-fashion brands sharing shelf space with streetwear labels. And if all the shopping gets a bit tiring, dive into the on-site Clarins spa for a rejuvenating massage – or even head there first to adequately prepare yourself for the retail adventure that lies in wait.
johnlewis.com

Menswear
Sharp suits and streetwear

①
Albam, Soho
Quality basics

James Shaw and Alastair Rae
launched Albam in 2006 in
response to the "distorted prices
for quality basics" prevalent in
the market. To achieve their goal
of simple, modern yet affordable
clothing they spent time sourcing
small factories and workshops,
mostly in the UK, which are now
growing along with Albam's retail.

The first shop opened in
Soho's Beak Street in 2006. Two
more followed respectively in
Old Spitalfields Market and on
Upper Street, within walking
distance of Angel Underground
station. The shops showcase the
full Albam collection of key
menswear pieces that, unlike
many brands, are launched at
the right time of year and work
for seasons to come.
23 Beak Street, W1F 9RS
+44 (0)20 3157 7000
albamclothing.com

TOP PICKS
01 Jeans by Albam
02 Running shoes by
     Nike Internationalist
03 City bike by London's
     Brother Cycles for Albam
04 Wax jacket by Albam
05 Custom-made rucksacks by
     Aiguille Alpine Equipment

On the up
Albam now
boasts three
shops in
London

② Private White VC, Mayfair
Military style

Inspired by the wardrobe of Victoria Cross recipient Private Jack White and born out of a devotion to genuine British manufacturing, this Manchester-based label turns out stylish, locally made workwear and military-influenced pieces. The second shop in London opened in late 2014 on Duke Street in Mayfair, joining the store on London's Lambs Conduit Street and the original shop in Manchester. The designs marry functionality and style to produce pieces that are simple, timeless and fantastically comfortable.
73 Duke Street, W1K 5NR
+ 44 (0)20 7629 9918
privatewhitevc.com

❸ Drake's, Hoxton
Neckwear to impress

When British tiemaker Drake's moved into its premises in Hoxton it wanted its clients to see the production steps for themselves. "We're not hiding the manufacturing process; in fact, we're celebrating it," says director Michael Hill.

Since 2013 the entire firm has occupied this open-plan building where up to 2,000 ties are made by the 20-strong staff each week. On the ground floor there is a snug retail space – the brand's second after its original shop just off Savile Row.

Only one of the seven stages of the production process involves the use of a machine; the rest are done by hand. "Drake's has always been about 'Made in London' so it would have been disingenuous if we hadn't been here," says Hill of the space, fittingly situated on Haberdasher Street in the East End.
3 Haberdasher Street, N1 6ED
+ 44 (0)20 7608 0321
drakes.com

④ Oliver Spencer, Bloomsbury
Challenging class

London's Lambs Conduit Street is a menswear stronghold that hosts a parade of credible independent stores including that of Oliver Spencer, who opened his shop here in 2006. Today behind its restored Victorian façade, Spencer's collection is hung among displays of butterflies and anatomical models. "I want it to be a cross between the Royal Geographical Society and a classroom: a little challenging," he says.

Spencer started in fashion in 1991 when he launched Favourbrook, a company specialising in traditional wedding garb. Over time, however, he started making very British clothing, often inspired by military and hunting outfits. This led to the launch of his eponymous line of menswear in 2002. The clothes are made in the UK and Portugal and most of the fabrics come from British mills. More recent additions to the brand include womenswear, shoes and eyewear. Mixed in with Spencer's collection in the shop in Bloomsbury are offerings by the likes of Il Bussetto, New Balance and Sunspel.
58 and 62 Lambs Conduit Street,
WC1N 3LW
+ 44 (0)20 7269 6444
oliverspencer.co.uk

British style is in great shape. Just like myself

There's a
lot of Lambs
Conduit
Street left so
pick up the
pace, officer

⑥
E Tautz, Mayfair
Contemporary tailoring

Patrick Grant, the man who almost
single-handedly revived Norton &
Sons and British bespoke tailoring
along with it, also restarted E Tautz
in 2009.

The pared-back Duke Street
store – complete with mid-century
furniture and wood-panelled walls
– opened in 2014 and houses a
ready-to-wear range and, downstairs,
the brand's tailoring service.

Meanwhile, those who would
rather head to the original home of
tailoring, Savile Row, should check
out Grant's first outpost Norton &
Sons at No 16.
71 Duke Street, W1K 5NX
+44 (0)20 7629 8809
etautz.com

⑦
Dunhill, Mayfair
Club-house classics

This Georgian mansion, once
the Duke of Westminster's London
residence and the only detached
house in Mayfair, is now the
spiritual home of Dunhill in the
British capital. A traditional
clubhouse atmosphere prevails
and you'll find a spa, barber
and even humidor here.

Alongside Dunhill's ready-to-
wear suits there is also a bespoke
tailoring service (the brand
recruited one of Savile Row's
master tailors, Martin Nicholls)
with more than 300 cloths for
suits and 450 fabrics for shirts
to choose from.

The bespoke service extends
beyond suiting to leather goods,
including suitcases, all handmade
in north London. If you can't
make it to Bourdon House,
Dunhill also has a smaller outpost
on Jermyn Street.
2 Davies Street, W1K 3DJ
+44 (0)20 7853 4440
dunhill.com

⑤
Universal Works, Bloomsbury
Utilitarian staples

After honing his trade at British
menswear designer Paul Smith and
Maharishi, David Keyte (*pictured*)
rolled out his inaugural Universal
Works menswear collection in 2009
on Lambs Conduit Street. Aimed
at men more concerned with clothes
that last rather than the latest fad,
the brand's shirts, trousers and
knitwear feel contemporary yet
grounded in a UK sensibility.
"The inspiration comes from a
blue-collar worker background,"
says Keyte, "but one that knows
how to dress and live well."
37 Lambs Conduit Street,
WC1N 3NG
+44 (0)20 3632 2115
universalworks.co.uk

Ⓐ
Anderson & Sheppard, Mayfair
Suits for any occasion

London tailor Anderson & Sheppard's shop on Clifford Street in Mayfair offers a comfortable environment for customers to discover beautiful pieces, from handmade Irish sweaters to trousers that are cut to fit every occasion. The haberdashery opened at the end of Savile Row in 2012 and only a few steps away from the workshop where bespoke suits are made for customers.

"Clifford Street is an addition to the atelier on Old Burlington Street," says owner Anda Rowland (*pictured, left*). "In the latter you can get a suit or jacket made up and in the new shop you can get everything else."
17 Clifford Street, W1S 3RQ
+ 44 (0)20 7287 7300;
32 Old Burlington Street, W1S 3AT
+ 44 (0)20 7734 1420
anderson-sheppard.co.uk

(1)

Mouki Mou, Marylebone
Handpicked treasures

Since 2013, Marylebone's Chiltern Street has had a new gem in its retail line-up: Mouki Mou, a womenswear and accessories boutique dedicated to beautiful items handpicked by Greek founder Maria Lemos. "The concept of the store is that of discovery," says Lemos. "That's why we've kept the cluster of small rooms below instead of creating one large space." The whitewashed venue was designed by Pentagram and is lined with Nordic pine flooring, Carrara marble and a black spiral steel staircase.

The collection represents more than 30 international brands, including clothing from 45RPM, pens from German stationery heavyweight Kaweco, Janaki Larsen ceramics and bags by Spanish designer Isaac Reina. There are about 20 independent jewellery brands on display from around the world: cuffs and necklaces by the likes of Jem from France, New York's Gabriella Kiss, Japan's Cherry Brown and Ileana Makri from Greece.

29 Chiltern Street, W1U 7PL
+44 (0)20 7224 4010
moukimou.com

Greek chic
—
Expect to see a touch of the owner's Med heritage

There's
a second
load to
pick up
yet

② Workshop, Islington
Multibrand mecca

The characterful cobbled Camden Passage in Islington is home to Workshop – an independent multibrand store owned by Turin-born, London-based siblings Aldo and Giulia Acchiardi. The venue opened in 2009 as a testing ground for Giulia's Harris Wharf London womenswear line of timeless fuss-free coats and dresses – made in the Acchiardi family's factory in Turin from Italian-sourced fabrics.

Besides the in-house line of subtle pieces, in the shop you can also find tops by Spanish label Masscob, bags by French-Italian T-L180 and Anniel flat shoes. In 2014 Workshop opened a second location in Notting Hill, just steps away from the buzzing Portobello Road.

19 Camden Passage, N1 8EA
+44 (0)20 7226 3141
workshop-london.co.uk

Giulia Acchiardi's favourite shops in London

01 Mouki Mou "This shop [*see opposite page*] on Marylebone's Chiltern Street has a great selection of jewellery." *moukimou.com*

02 Smug "A beautiful homeware boutique two doors down from our shop on Camden Passage." *ifeelsmug.com*

03 Strut "Great for pre-owned designer clothing." *strutlondon.com*

04 Dover Street Market "A must-visit with an international selection of brands." *doverstreetmarket.com*

05 Liberty "With stylish decor and a smart selection of women's brands, it's a great Soho shopping stop." *liberty.co.uk*

East and west
—
As well as five London shops there's one in Tokyo, too

④
J&M Davidson, Notting Hill
Japanese-approved leatherwear

John and Monique Davidson (*pictured*) started making leather belts in 1984, which were soon followed by a full range of accessories and – since 1997 – womenswear. The wooden shelves in the Golborne Road shop in Notting Hill display the duo's bags, shoes and belts, featuring high-quality hides and intricate hand-stitching; elegant, easy-to-wear garments hang from the rails. Most bags and wallets are handcrafted in Spain or Italy and clothes are made in Japan, where the brand has been present since 1984.

J&M Davidson opened a second location in Tokyo's Aoyama in late 2012. It's a canny addition to its stable given that Japan is its biggest international market.
97 Golborne Road,W10 5NL
+ 44 (0)20 8969 2244
jandmdavidson.com

③
MHL, Marylebone
Androgynous appeal

After the success of the Shoreditch establishment, Margaret Howell picked New Cavendish Street in Marylebone for MHL's (the company's diffusion range) second London base. The Margaret Howell brand's ascendancy is mostly due to its popularity in Japan but its essence remains British: lambswool, tweed and Scottish cashmere are some of its signature textiles. And despite a refined main line, the MHL trademark is utility. "Part of the style is a sort of androgyny – an equality based on a lifestyle where one is active and works," says Howell.
22 New Cavendish Street,W1G 8TT
+ 44 (0)20 7487 3803
margarethowell.co.uk

I'll definitely grow into these

His and hers
Sunspel's womenswear line launched in 2011

⑤ Celestine Eleven, Shoreditch
Alternative clothing

Working with London-based interior designer Morse Studio, Tena Strok opened her Celestine Eleven womenswear in 2013. The roomy space in Shoreditch winningly combines untreated plaster walls and reclaimed wood counters with sleek shelves and even sleeker furniture.

Dresses by Meadham Kirchhoff and Marios Schwab, tops by Rika and knitwear by Theyskens' Theory barely have time to hang on copper-plated pipes before they are snapped up. The library section has titles on cooking, photography and fashion while the apothecary section has skincare by Alexandra Soveral and Sort of Coal. "We want to pair focused fashion and elements of alternative living," says Strok, whose shop also offers alternative therapies such as reiki massage sessions should you fancy them.
4 Holywell Lane, EC2A 3ET
+44 (0)20 7729 2987
celestineeleven.com

TOP PICKS
01 Soaps by Sort of Coal
02 Hats by Wendy Nichol
03 Boots by Penelope Chilvers
04 Floral tops by Cecile
05 Dresses by Lucas Nascimento

⑥ Sunspel, Marylebone
Heritage-led womenswear

It has been over 60 years since British underwear and T-shirt label Sunspel introduced its two-ply Egyptian-cotton boxer shorts to the discerning English gentleman. In 2011 the Brit brand launched its first women's collection, offering modern must-haves and basics such as Egyptian cotton polo dresses, tank tops and skirts.

With six shops in London and one in Melbourne, the brand continues to celebrate its "Made in England" heritage. The shop on Chiltern Street in Marylebone carries Sunspel's full range of men's and women's basics, all made in the factory in Long Eaton near Nottingham.

The business is enjoying a period of growth and is proving popular among a new loyal set of followers. It has certainly enjoyed a new lease of life since being purchased in 2005 by Dominic Hazelhurst and Nicholas Brooke.

"What attracted us to the business was the extraordinary level of customer loyalty to the brand and its Englishness, which still carries resonance internationally," says Hazelhurst.
13-15 Chiltern Street, W1U 7PG
+44 (0)20 7009 0650
sunspel.com

Sole trader
—
Shoe Corner
offers 8,000
pairs of
shoes

⑦
Fenwick, Mayfair
The all-in-one experience

Family-owned Fenwick's Bond Street flagship has been around since 1891. In 2013, the retailer (with 11 locations across the UK) was given a facelift by Selfridges veteran David Walker-Smith, with a major focus on womenswear.

This multibrand boutique now stocks a wide range of footwear from Acne to Valentino and clothing from the likes of Sofie d'Hoore and Isabel Marant. And when those shopping bags begin to weigh you down, treat yourself to a massage at Blink's spa or afternoon tea at in-house restaurant Bond & Brook.
63 New Bond Street, W1S 1RQ
+44 (0)20 7629 9161
fenwick.co.uk

⑧
Egg Trading, Belgravia
Breaking the mould

Tucked among the whitewashed residences in Belgravia in a flat-turned-workshop is Maureen Doherty's Egg Trading clothing shop. Its central location suits an international customer base, allowing for an easy stopover when buyers fly into town. Focusing primarily on womenswear, the venue also offers handcrafted ceramics, linens and home accessories.

The idea for Egg was hatched from an animosity towards the constant urge for change within the fashion industry. Working for years in the textile rush (including more than a decade spent at Issey Miyake), Doherty decided to break with tradition. "I wanted to open a space that sold clothes as one would buy a table: as something special that could last for at least a decade," she says.
36 Kinnerton Street, SW1X 8ES
+44 (0)20 7235 9315
eggtrading.com

TOP PICKS
01   Handmade shoes by
         Le Yucca's
02   Sweaters by Sine Fiennes
03   Basics by Apunto B
04   Womenswear designed
         in-house by Egg

⑨
Anna, Primrose Hill
Upmarket womenswear

After a leisurely stroll around Primrose Hill, step into the two-storey flagship location of Anna Park's womenswear boutiques, one of six branches across the country.

The light-flooded bare-brick space showcases a stylish fusion of established fashion staples as well as up-and-coming designers from around the world. Shop here for denim from Current/Elliott and Rag & Bone, dresses by Acne Studios and Diane von Furstenberg, and outerwear from Woolrich.
126 Regents Park Road, NW1 8XL
+44 (0)20 7483 0411
shopatanna.com

Homeware
Interior motives

1

Native & Co, Notting Hill
Eastern promise

Product designers Sharon Hung and Chris Green (*pictured*) launched the bricks-and-mortar version of their online shop Native & Co in Notting Hill in 2014. The spartan, minimalist design of the shop floor belies the comprehensive range of home and tableware, such as handmade canvas and leather totes, linen throws and enamel coffee pots. The majority of items – made by artisans in Japan and Taiwan – can't be found elsewhere in Europe.

"We've picked all these products on our travels," says Hung. "It's about contemporary aesthetics using traditional techniques."
116 Kensington Park Road,
W11 2PW
+44 (0)20 7243 0418
nativeandco.com

2

Vitsoe, Marylebone
Part of the furniture

Vitsoe's shop in Marylebone is London's retail outpost of the eponymous furniture company set up by Niels Vitsoe alongside Otto Zapf in 1959, to conceive and distribute the designs of German designer Dieter Rams. Behind its brick façade the shop sells Rams' signature 606 Universal Shelving System, the 620 Chair Programme and 621 side table. Since 1995 the company's headquarters and production have been based in London with additional shops to be found in New York, Los Angeles and Munich.
3-5 Duke Street, W1U 3ED
+44 (0)20 7428 1606
vitsoe.com

3

SCP, Shoreditch
Classic know-how

In operation for 30 years, SCP has a reputation for being one of London's finest design shops. Charismatic founder Sheridan Coakley set out to produce new designs in the spirit of the modern movement and the large retail space in Shoreditch contains a plentiful range that still keeps this design reference. A Britishness fused with a Scandinavian sensibility defines SCP's style, with designers such as Donna Wilson and Reiko Kaneko offering a lightness of touch and aesthetic that is driven by durability and function.
135-139 Curtain Road, EC2A 3BX
+44 (0)20 7739 1869
scp.co.uk

Don't you find that impeccable style is immediately obvious?

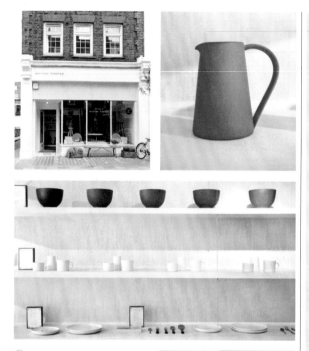

④

Another Country, Marylebone
Devils for detail

Having joined Marylebone's lively
retail scene in 2014, furniture
designer-turned-entrepreneur Paul
de Zwart's Another Country has
swiftly become the must-visit design
shop in the area. "In terms of
texture, lines and timber finish, the
store reflects our brand," says De
Zwart. "We're big on detail like our
brass fixtures; the things that matter
in furniture matter in the store."

The two-level showroom focuses
on wooden products of certified,
sustainable provenance. Eight
designers work on the brand's
seasonal collections that have
recently grown to include textiles
and lights. Sitting alongside their
creations in the airy, cream- coloured
rooms are what the brand calls
"evergreen" products: design staples
from the likes of David Mellor (*see
opposite page*), Ian McIntyre and
Belgium's Le Typographe.
*18 Crawford Street,W1H 1BT
+44 (0)20 7486 3251
anothercountry.com*

Vintage furniture

London has been hailed as the
world's design capital and its
maze of streets is filled with
gems if you're looking for mid-
20th century vintage furniture.
Here are some top picks.

01 Forest London, Islington:
Dutch design aficionado
Eva Coppens's beautiful
space in north London is
dedicated to Scandinavian
and northern European
vintage furniture,
homeware and lighting.
It is mixed and matched
with contemporary
collaborations and
accessories such as the
in-house Forest Cushion
collection, handmade in
the UK.
forestlondon.com

02 Chase & Sorensen,
Dalston: Walk down
Dalston Lane and you'll
come across this treasure
trove of classic mid-20th
century Scandinavian
furniture and decorations.
The walls, sideboards and
tables are decked with
accessories from Royal
Copenhagen to Frama;
vintage items from the
likes of Hans J Wegner and
Børge Mogensen are also
shipped in straight from
Denmark every few weeks.
chaseandsorensen.com

03 The Peanut Vendor,
Islington: This
2008-established shop
has its eye on design
classics from Bauhaus-
era Bakelite lamps to
Jan Vanek's chairs and
Robert Heal's 1964
Ladderax modular
shelving system. Among
these you will also find
vintage gifts and a library
of books for design
enthusiasts, including
Dominic Bradbury's must-
read *Mid-Century Modern*.
thepeanutvendor.co.uk

⑤ Folklore, Islington
Form and function

Danielle and Bob Reid opened design shop Folklore on Islington's bustling Upper Street in 2012 with the commendable aim of creating better living through clean and practical modern design. "Our focus is on materials, process and source," says Bob of their range of homeware, furniture and lighting. "We are drawn to functional goods that are created with care."

Stone-made tableware by the venture's own collection sits next to handcrafted brushes from Swedish brand Iris Hantverk, while squid-ink-stained furniture made in collaboration with Cornwall-based designer Felix McCormack adorns the interior. There are also organic-cotton linens by small producers across Europe and skincare products from Denver-based Fig+Yarrow.
193 Upper Street, N1 1RQ
+44 (0)20 7354 9333
shopfolklore.com

⑥ David Mellor, Chelsea
Cutting-edge cutlery

David Mellor's cutlery has become one of the staples of British design (*see our essay on page 89*). All pieces are manufactured in a purpose-built factory in the Peak District National Park in Derbyshire while the shop in Sloane Square stocks a wide range of selected pieces to fill your kitchen. That includes everything from fine bone china by the late Mellor himself to teapots from Marimekko and kettles by Michael Graves for Alessi.
4 Sloane Square, SW1W 8EE
+44 (0)20 7730 4259
davidmellordesign.com

⑦ TwentyTwentyOne, Islington
Past meets present

This is a brand that has one foot in the modernist history of the past century and the other firmly in the contemporary trends of today. Founders Simon Alderson and Tony Cunningham are constantly on the hunt for the best in emerging design and established classics. The result is an enticingly eclectic collection that spans all aspects of furniture and homeware. The shop, located on Upper Street in Islington, is a treasure trove of discoveries waiting to be found. Meanwhile, the lofty showroom on River Street displays all manner of pieces from the several hundred designers that TwentyTwentyOne stocks.
274-275 Upper Street, N1 2UA
+44 (0)20 7288 1996
twentytwentyone.com

⑧ The New Craftsmen, Mayfair
Artisan network

The New Craftsmen has quickly emerged as London's must-visit design concept store. Offering a selection of the UK's finest craft-makers, the collection is a testament to the rising standard of design and products made on these shores. Founded in 2012 as a "network" as much as a retail venture, more than 70 makers are represented, all with the common thread of exactingly high quality. The shop in Mayfair opened its doors in 2014 in a 19th-century former leather-breeches workshop.

From sturdy chairs by Gareth Neal to quirky ceramics from Nicola Tassie there is no better place in London to buy British craft under one roof. Regular "atelier" events give more studious visitors the chance to learn some of the tricks of the trade with the makers themselves.
34 North Row, W1K 6DG
+44 (0)20 7148 3190
thenewcraftsmen.com

⑨ Jasper Morrison, Dalston
Celebrating normality

It is little wonder that when one of Britain's most acclaimed industrial and product designers decided to open a shop in 2011 it turned out to be good. Jasper Morrison's retail space is part of the designer's former studio and is placed ever so discreetly on a shabby, unassuming stretch of Kingsland Road.

Anonymity and a celebration of normality are big drivers for Morrison and this is reflected directly in the store, which lives and breathes good taste in everything it stocks.

Many items are left to speak for themselves and an anti-big-name-designer philosophy dominates. Among the favourites are Rex potato peelers from Switzerland, Fiskars scissors from Finland and a folding tray table by Hans J Wegner from Denmark.
24B Kingsland Road, E2 8DA
jaspermorrisonshop.com

10
Momosan, Hackney
Global vision

Japanese homeware might be the main star of this tiny retail space in Hackney's quiet Wilton Way but owner Momoko Mizutani (*pictured*) has created connections and inventive links between the two countries she chose to call home. The shelves display her collection of traditional Nippon pottery and "Made in Britain" gems such as tealight holders.

With a touch of further international diversity from Dutch brass lamps to wooden toys from Austria, the selection has an assorted heritage but is brought together by Mizutani's attention to ethical production and careful handicraft.
79A Wilton Way, E8 1BG
momosanshop.com

TOP PICKS
01   Wooden bowls by
        Kihachi Kobo
02   Stools by Riki Watanabe
03   Tealight holders by Momosan

11
Labour and Wait, Shoreditch
Timeless classics

Owners and former menswear designers Rachel Wythe-Moran and Simon Watkins opened their first Labour and Wait homeware shop in 2000 and moved into the current (and larger) location in a former pub in Shoreditch a decade later.

"We have sourced a collection of everyday classics that will not date but will mellow and improve with age," says Wythe-Moran. Although the duo look all over the world to source products such as Alfonso Bialetti espresso makers and Couto toothpaste from Portugal, they manufacture some items locally, including an in-house range of aprons, kitchen towels and handkerchiefs. Everything they sell is intended to bring added pleasure to life's daily routines.
85 Redchurch Street, E2 7DJ
+44 (0)20 7729 6253
labourandwait.co.uk

There's a fine line between quality shopping and getting airborne

Ⓘ
Brooks England, Covent Garden
Best for cycling accessories

BI866 opened in early 2014 and is Brooks England's first flagship shop in London's Covent Garden. Iron-and-copper shelving showcases the brand's latest cycling accessories and 50 different styles of saddles, including the sought-after Cambium line made from vulcanised rubber and organic-cotton canvas. It's the only place in the world to carry the complete range of Brooks saddles and bags. The space also sells the brand's famous Barbican Leather Legacy bags alongside Land's End and John O'Groats panniers.
36 Earlham Street, WC2H 9LH
+44 (0)20 7836 9968
b1866.com

②
Claire Goldsmith, Notting Hill
Raise your glasses

Back in the day, Oliver Goldsmith framed the faces of Audrey Hepburn, Grace Kelly, Michael Caine and other household names with his iconic spectacles and sunglasses. Since 2010 his great-granddaughter Claire has been continuing the family tradition with her own eyewear line.

Each pair of glasses is handmade in the UK. The complete collections of Claire Goldsmith frames can be found in this Notting Hill shop while some of Oliver's most cherished models are displayed in the archives in the basement.
15 All Saints Road, W11 1HA
+44 (0)20 7460 0844
clairegoldsmith.com

③
By Appointment Only Design, Marylebone
Forward-thinking florists

Tucked away on Chiltern Street is By Appointment Only Design's flower shop. Inside you'll find blossoms, candles and gifts, and a team of florists whose creative bouquets have decorated the halls of countless homes and venues including Claridge's. The team has no geographical boundaries and has assisted clients across Europe to host the perfect party. The floral displays are inspired by the seasons and London's cultural riches. A perfect place for same-day flower deliveries within London.
38 Chiltern Street, W1U 7QL
+44 (0)20 7486 7870
byappointmentonlydesign.com

④
NikeLab 1948, Shoreditch
Unique sneakers

What sets the Shoreditch NikeLab apart from its sister retailers is that the space has been built to match the company's design principles: innovation, sustainability and functionality. Nestled under railway arches, it sports a laser installation by London-based artist group Marshmallow Laser Feast. The kicks are still the main attraction: a selection of the latest and most innovative Nike trainers are treated like art and prominently displayed. Multilingual staff are here to help you navigate a range that includes pairs that can't be found elsewhere.
477/478 Bateman's Row, EC2A 3HH
+44 (0)20 7729 7688
nike.com

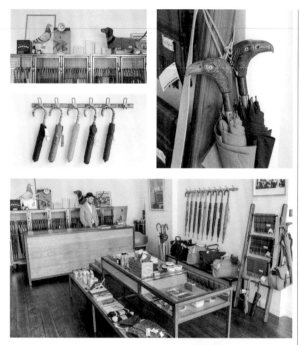

6

William & Son, Mayfair
Royally approved gifts

Mayfair is the home of high-end retailer William & Son, which has been selling luxury goods from jewellery and watches to leather accessories and handmade game sets since 1999. The family-run business was founded by William Asprey (a member of the Asprey family, the UK's centuries-old jewellery maker) and prizes authentic British artisanship. In 2009 it received a Royal Warrant by way of recognition for the quality of its goldsmiths' and silversmiths' work.

Exclusively designed glassware by the likes of Anna Torfs and William Yeoward is also available. If chess and dominoes are your thing you can have a set made to order by one of William & Son's craftsmen. If getting married is your thing, the shop also takes orders for wedding rings.
34-36 Bruton Street, W1J 6QX
+44 (0)20 7493 8385
williamandson.com

5

London Undercover, Spitalfields
Best for brollies

Jamie Milestone's wish to celebrate the umbrella as the ultimate British fashion accessory came true when he opened London Undercover in 2008. The shop in east London sells a range of elegant yet durable umbrellas (think heavy-duty steel frames on solid beech or bamboo-cane sticks) that are nothing like the disposable and essentially useless black brollies that are sold on many rainy street corners in London's more touristy spots.

Milestone (*pictured*) has luxurious offerings for men and women that are handcrafted in the UK using nothing but the finest eco-friendly materials. London Undercover not only sells its own creations but also collaborates with designers such as Timothy Everest to create expressive patterns that are guaranteed to bring a splash of colour to a drizzly day.
20 Hanbury Street, E1 6QR
+44 (0)20 7482 4321
londonundercover.co.uk

7

Honeyjam, Notting Hill
Traditional playtime

Determined to buck the trend of children being distracted by the glowing screens of smartphones, Honey Bowdrey and Jasmine Guinness opened the doors to their traditional Notting Hill toyshop in 2006. "We were inspired by our own childhood memories of toyshops crammed with the most marvellous things," says Bowdrey.

Although there is no lack of contemporary playthings in Honeyjam, the shop specialises in original, old-school toys such as plastic army soldiers, teddy bears, wooden animals and pick-up sticks.
2 Blenheim Crescent, W11 1NN
+44 (0)20 7243 0449
honeyjam.co.uk

⑧ Smythson, Chelsea
Leather expert of note

Smythson's luxurious stationery, bags and leather accessories have been charming London since 1887 and the brand counts the royal family among its clients. Its Sloane Street location opened in 2013: a two-storey shop sporting shelves stacked with classic briefcases in leathers including calfskin, crocodile and python. The company is also renowned for its pocket-sized notebooks designed by founder Frank Smythson. Customers can add a personal touch by having their name engraved or embossed on their purchases.
141-142 Sloane Street, SW1X 9AY
+ 44 (0)20 7730 5520
smythson.com

⑨ Present & Correct, Islington
Stationery to write home about

Set in Islington's Arlington Way, Present & Correct is a must-stop for stationery obsessives. Opened in 2012 by graphic designer Neal Whittington, the space sells everything from notebooks and postcards to giftwrap and German invoice pads.
"Most of our customers are artists and designers or connected to those circles," says Whittington. "However, we are becoming a destination for shoppers on the lookout for unusual gifts." Most of the items are designed by Whittington; the rest are sourced from his overseas travels.
23 Arlington Way, EC1R 1UY
+ 44 (0)20 7278 2460
presentandcorrect.com

Record shops
Cover stars

① Kristina Records, Dalston
Discerning disk vendors

Those looking for Kristina Records in Dalston may have a hard time: it's unsigned and unbranded (at least on the outside). This outlet for well-selected vinyl with a lean towards underground dance music offers a welcoming space to flip through the racks. You can also flip out at some world-class DJ talent as the shop regularly holds sets from top musicians.
"You get a mix of DJs and artists and that's one of the attractions of any record shop," says co-founder Jason Spinks. "You could walk in here and find [house-music legend] Theo Parrish playing records. I've also seen people meet here and form strong friendships."
Wander in and ask the knowledgeable staff what's hot. Spinks' tips? Local labels OdD Music and LB Produce.
44 Stoke Newington Road, N16 7XJ
+ 44 (0)20 7254 2130
kristinarecords.com

Three more

01 Phonica, Soho: Half shop, half well-appointed lounge (like a friend's place – a friend with really good taste), Phonica opened in 2003 and has gone from strength to strength. It's a purveyor of well-selected vinyl catering to lovers of anything from minimal techno to indulgent disco.
phonicarecords.com

02 Sister Ray, Soho: An indie-music institution, Sister Ray's offerings can now be bought at its second location in London's Ace Hotel. Its heart remains distinctly in the garage with guitars, intelligent pop and dance music on offer.
sisterray.co.uk

03 Rough Trade, citywide: The shop and the record label, born in the 1970s, parted ways some years back but still share Rough Trade's reputation as vendor of all that's fresh and interesting about the London music scene. You could start at Rough Trade's west London store to get a taste of where the story started. But its newer east London location has a more energetic buzz and does great coffee.
roughtrade.com

Bookshops
Top reads

①
Daunt Books, Marylebone
Bookseller with pedigree

Daunt Books is a Marylebone institution (it also has branches citywide). The building dates back to 1910 and is the oldest purpose-built bookshop in the capital. The interior is like stepping into a time warp: oak galleries, lofty skylights and a huge stained-glass window. "The shop was founded on the idea of arranging books by country rather than genre," says manager Brett Wolstencroft. This is still the case; in the cavernous back room, travel, literature and history titles sit under broad regional and country categories.
*83 Marylebone High Street,
W1U 4QW
+44 (0)20 7224 2295
dauntbooks.co.uk*

Four more

01 Koenig Books, citywide: One of three London branches of German chain Walther Koenig Books (the other two being in the Whitechapel Gallery and the Serpentine Gallery), the Charing Cross shop specialises in books on photography, art and architecture. *buchhandlung-walther-koenig.de*

02 Foyles, Soho: Opened its flagship store on Charing Cross Road in 2014. Designed by architecture studio Lifschutz Davidson Sandilands, the space used to be the home of Central Saint Martins art school – now it houses more than 200,000 titles. *foyles.co.uk*

03 Hatchards, Piccadilly: The oldest surviving bookshop in the capital dates back to 1797 when it was founded by John Hatchard (his portrait still hangs on the wall). Look out for signed editions. *hatchards.co.uk*

04 Donlon Books, Broadway Market: Specialises in art and culture, including titles on photography and interior design as well as independent magazines. *donlonbooks.com*

Street markets
Slice of life

①
Best markets
Outdoor shopping

London is not only abundant in farmers' markets (*see the Food and drink section from page 28*), the capital is also rich with bazaars selling a cornucopia of vintage finds, great furnishings, books and quirky accessories. Whether it's the bohemian (albeit at times too touristy) ❶*Portobello Market* in Notting Hill for antiques or the ❷*Broadway Market* along the Regent's Canal in Hackney, offering everything from art publications and prints (Donlon Books) to cycle accessories (Lock 7 Cycle Cafe) and world-cinema DVD rentals (The Film Shop), the capital's markets boast a kaleidoscope of tastes and cultures. (Don't forget to try the fantastic food on offer at Broadway, too.)

There is of course, the lavishly green ❸*Columbia Road Flower Market*. Set on the edge of Shoreditch in the East End, the street blossoms on Sunday mornings with everything from bedding plants to banana plants up for grabs. Besides sumptuous flowers and greenery, Columbia Road is home to 60 independent retailers and art galleries.

Meanwhile for the most discerning of design and furniture tastes there is ❹*Alfies Antique Market* on the eastern end of Church Street in St John's Wood. Opened in 1976, today the art deco building houses around 100 antique dealers and a rooftop café. Plus there are some 20 additional shops selling mid-century antiques nearby on Church Street, including the very nice James Worrall. If you don't have time for all of them, check out Decoratum – one of Europe's largest commercial galleries specialising in lighting – or Renato Ferrari for glass and ceramics. Either way the chances are you won't leave empty-handed.

Where to find them

01 Portobello Market: Portobello Road, W10 5TA
+44 (0)20 7727 7684
portobelloroad.co.uk

02 Broadway Market: E8 4QJ
+44 (0)7709 311 869
broadwaymarket.co.uk

03 Columbia Road Flower Market: Columbia Road, E2 7RG
columbiaroad.info

04 Alfies Antique Market: 13-25 Church Street, NW8 8DT
+44 (0)20 7723 6066
alfiesantiques.com

Things we'd buy
—— Top capital take-homes

No trip to London should be considered fulfilled if you don't manage to bag some of the capital's finest offerings. That could be special-edition vinyl by home-grown talent, stylish prints from the London Transport Museum or how about intricate homeware and accessories from switched-on designers? Whether it's a classic hand-stitched tie, a chic yet sturdy umbrella, or, for the food fans among you, traditional biscuits and aromatic teas, here is our selection of the best products to take with you when leaving the city.

And who knew that some of Europe's finest bubbly in the past decade or so comes from England? (Now you do.) Whether a treat for yourself or a gift for your nearest and dearest, the products on our list will make the perfect souvenir of your visit to the capital.

01 Ties by Drake's
drakes.com
02 Rainproof coat by Mackintosh
mackintosh.com
03 Umbrella by London Undercover
londonundercover.co.uk
04 Pet accessories by Mungo & Maud
mungoandmaud.com
05 Candle holders by Marie Dessuant for Another Country
anothercountry.com
06 Purses by Ettinger
ettinger.co.uk
07 Model of Farringdon Station by Chisel & Mouse
chiselandmouse.com
08 Wooden blocks by Miller Goodman from SCP
scp.co.uk
09 Shoes by Crockett & Jones
crockettandjones.com
10 Accordion pocket notebooks by Monocle
monocle.com
11 Cashmere scarf by Johnstons of Elgin
johnstonscashmere.com
12 Silk scarf by Jane Carr
jane-carr.com
13 Dry gin by Sipsmith
sipsmith.com
14 Framed 'Touch' print by John Stezaker from Counter Editions
countereditions.com

01 Tea cups by People Will Always Need Plates peoplewill alwaysneedplates.co.uk
02 London Zoo poster by Abram Games from the London Transport Museum ltmuseumshop.co.uk
03 Biscuits by Cartwright & Butler from Selfridges selfridges.com

04 No 89 Eau de Toilette by Floris florislondon.com
05 Limited-edition books and records by The Vinyl Factory vfeditions.com
06 Fine tea blends by Postcard Teas in Mayfair postcardteas.com
07 Chapel Down vintage reserve English sparkling wine chapeldown.com

08 Blanket by Eleanor Pritchard × Trunk from Trunk Clothiers trunkclothiers.com
09 *A Murder of Quality* by John le Carré from Penguin Books and *The Mask of Dimitrios* by Eric Ambler from The Folio Society penguin.co.uk; foliosociety.com

12 essays
—— Urban exploration

Now for a bird's-eye view of the city

ESSAY 01

Clean and serene
Wild parks and
lofty gardens

It may be hard to believe
amid the steel-and-glass
towers of the City or the
bars of east London but
you are in one of the
most verdant capitals in
the world. Almost half of
the city is green space,
from manicured, flower-
bedded spaces to wooded
idylls just steps from an
Underground station.

by Ben Olsen,
Monocle

Beyond its iconic skyline, blockbuster
galleries and ubiquitous grey skies – plus
that family who live in Buckingham
Palace – London's lesser-known claim
to fame is its position among the world's
greenest cities. Celebrated in 1990s anthem
"Parklife" by indie stalwarts Blur – its lyrics
joyously depicting Londoners dodging the
rat race, feeding the sparrows and cutting
down on their "pork life" to get some
exercise among the city's green spaces –
the turf-clad parks of the capital always
figure highly on our weekend agenda.

London doesn't offer respite by the
sea or solace atop a nearby mountain. So
the city's wilder spots – and the chance
to kick through leaves, breathe fresh air
and justify dog ownership – are as good a

tonic as it gets for an eight-million-strong
population renowned for being uptight.
It hardly needs science to link these green
spaces to happiness; a midsummer visit
to any of London's parks would draw a
casual observer to the same conclusion.
Still, a 2013 academic study found that,
regardless of income, class or marital
status, proximity to the great outdoors
saw virtually all respondents report
higher life satisfaction. Luckily, with 47
per cent of the city – from royal parks to
rejuvenated nature reserves – classified
as "green", there is certainly plenty to
choose from.

Trophy parks include Hampstead
Heath – a wide-and-wild expanse with
knockout city views from its upper reaches,
ponds you can swim in and parakeets
– and Regent's Park, where amid 160
hecatres of gardens, lakes and green spaces
you can find 12,000 roses, 100 wild-bird
species and a wide variety of team sport.
Only slightly more feral are the goings-
on at neighbouring London Zoo, where
passers-by can glimpse what's happening
on the towering Baboon Mountain.

South of the river the stately
Greenwich Park – home to the Royal
Observatory and the former benchmark
of global time – has museums, markets
and an award-winning brewery on its
doorstep. London's long summer days
allow time for post-work picnics while
spring's emerging daffodils, autumn's
technicoloured leaf fall and the occasional
dusting of snow in winter provide a
backdrop for a revolving cast of park
dwellers. And beyond nature's seasonal
comings and
goings you'll find
contemporary-
art fairs (Frieze),
musical
heavyweights
(Lovebox Festival)
and a touch of
Shakespeare
(Regent's Park
Open Air Theatre)

"Long summer
days, spring
daffodils,
autumn leaf-fall
and winter snow
are the backdrop
for a revolving
cast of park
dwellers"

East London's
great green spaces
—
01 Clissold Park,
Stoke Newington
Biodomes and a petting zoo.
02 Hackney City Farm
For being at one with nature.
03 Springfield Park, Clapton
Canal-bordered, contoured
gem with great views and
a towpath café.

among those events creating a buzz in the city's parkland.

Yet London's greater green spaces often lie beyond the major parks that circle the city centre. Previously unloved infrastructure conceals places to connect with nature in far less manicured environs. There's the regeneration of Regent's Canal, for example. Running from Paddington to Limehouse via Camden, Angel and Hackney, it has seen the Victorian-era network of locks and towpaths transformed from poorly maintained blackspots to vibrant hangouts – complete with floating cafés, libraries, florists and cinemas – and convenient routeways for Flyknit-toting runners.

Another former transport link reborn is the disused railway line between Finsbury Park and Highgate. It is now a serene tree-lined amble favoured by dog-walkers, dating couples and day-trippers, who can reward their efforts with a visit to one of Highgate's olde-worlde pubs. This walk will also deliver you close to the atmospheric Highgate Cemetery, resting place of Karl Marx and one of London's Magnificent Seven cemeteries.

Not that all of London's natural spots are static sites of preservation: expect to discover innovative green spaces evolving in unusual places. Right in the heart of the chrome-and-glass-clad City you'll find the Sky Garden. Situated 160 metres above ground level at the top of Rafael Viñoly's so-called Walkie Talkie building, this landscaped garden in the heavens is open to the public and comes with vertigo-inducing views of the River Thames. Meanwhile, beyond a series of plans intended to replicate New York's High Line, one idea set to become reality is architect Thomas Heatherwick's "garden bridge" over the Thames that will connect north and south London. Dedicated to trees and gardens and billed as a site of leisure with little improvement to the transport network intended, it is living proof that city architects are increasingly keen to green their plans.

And it's not just the planners. The rise and rise of the vertical garden – adorning everything from gastropubs to US retailers J.Crew and Anthropologie's stores – has become part of London's urban design language. And the city's population is taking control at ground level, too. It started with guerrilla gardening – stealth floral transformations of drab roundabouts and roadsides – and has evolved to community-based pocket-park projects and the revival of the old-fashioned allotment.

In line with the rise of the organic movement, swathes of Londoners have embraced a new grow-your-own ethos. Be it beehives on rooftops, vegetables growing on windowsills or flower-bedecked frontages blooming across suburbia, this groundswell of city greening is helping to bring even more colour and life to the urban landscape. Now that truly is something to sing about. — (M)

ABOUT THE WRITER: Ben Olsen is a MONOCLE writer. Originally from the "middle of nowhere" in southwest England, braving London's great outdoors for his essay was a breeze. Apart from his narrow escape from Regent's Park's rowdy community of geese.

ESSAY 02
Put your wallet away
Priceless museums

———

Culture is commodified almost everywhere but London's great museums and galleries don't ask for a penny when you drop in. It's a liberating experience to be set free among such treasures. So if a visit to the café or gift shop beckons, knock yourself out – you'll be helping the greatest shows on Earth to keep saying, 'This one's on us.'

by Robert Bound,
Monocle

This little book lists hundreds of ways to spend your money in this dirty old town but the best tip of all might be to point you in the direction of what's free. Those perfumed boutiques will come on all coquettish to swipe your shekels. The maître d' at that smart restaurant will feign a long-lost fraternity as he eases you into your chair (and eases those notes from your purse) but in London, as in the none-more-germane harmonising of Luther Vandross and Janet Jackson, the best things in life really are free.

Of course, there's the great free show of the streets themselves. Walk and explore and play spot-the-difference between Hackney and Chelsea or wonder how the rolling green acres of Richmond and Hampstead can feel so different; stroll the canals, stride the parks and breathe the cool, fresh(ish) air. These are things to be cherished but they are as rude mechanicals in our play, our complimentary carnival of London. That free-ness means freedom and the stars of this free show are the museums.

"In London's free museums you don't have to get your money's worth: you can revisit that piece every day if the mood takes you"

Everywhere else your freedom is restricted by entrance fees but in London you can make like a millionaire at an auction and be intensely relaxed about being in a room full of valuable things. At the British Museum you'll have the freedom to scrutinise the Rosetta Stone; at the National Gallery you can compare Turner's "The Fighting Temeraire" with the ripples and shadows of the Thames itself. For the same price (no price) at the V&A you'll get an eyeful of Ossie Clark's Jagger-hugging catsuit for even fewer notes than you could stuff down the front of it; or maybe you'll let Tates Britain and Modern slug it out for your affections as they pull faces at each other from either side of the Thames. And it'll all cost you nothing but shoe leather. Or the fee-plus-tip for the limousine and driver you hired for the day you flash bastards (no wonder you're intensely relaxed in rooms full of loot).

Freeness and the freedom that it offers makes everyone feel sexy. Tourists might well make the London Eye go round but these wonderful free museums are only full of wonder because people have learnt to draw in them and can spend all day scrutinising the subtleties of Holbein's "The Ambassadors". Next time you see a peacoat and a pallid complexion sketching cross-legged on the polished parquet, try to buy their picture. Whether they end up as the new Van Dyck, Van Eyck, Van Gogh or van driver, you'll still have got most of that day's visual stimulation free of charge.

The expensive financing of these free museums is made up of a pennywise patchwork of government funding, lottery money, philanthropic gifts and the

good old museum gift shop. Just as Vermeer might have perfected the use of light, so London's museums have perfected the art of lightening your wallet by nudging you in the small of the back and wondering if you'd like to buy the postcard or the tea towel or the umbrella or the drinks coaster. Or the jigsaw puzzle and the fridge magnet? The pen, then? And surely the toothpick holder in the shape of a tree (thank you, the V&A).

I've heard people who've just seen the best works by Canaletto, Cézanne and Michelangelo complain that they've somehow been duped into concluding their gratis grand tour of art treasures in the gift shop (I hope that wasn't you). Don't let them leave without buying a set of six coffee cups decorated with Constable's clouds, I say. March them straight to the cash register with a Paul Nash tea tray and a pair of Hogarth oven gloves for good measure.

Living in London, I find it surprising to have to pay at the Louvre, the Prado, the Met. How lucky London is to live in relative ignorance of the realities of funding these great institutions. It's intolerable to spend much time in places where everything costs something *all the time*. But there's succour and security in a city where, in some small way, you don't have to feel you must get your money's worth – where you can look and linger and revisit

Best museums

—

01 Leighton House Museum, Holland Park
Former home of artist Lord Frederick Leighton.
02 Museum of Brands, Packaging & Advertising, Notting Hill
All things product design.
03 HMS Belfast, Southwark
Museum warship.

that piece every day if the mood takes you, like that tragic blonde in *Vertigo*.

Freeness and the freedom that it offers are precious but precarious. Priceless paintings presented in stunning surroundings on show for nothing? That is a delicate illusion to maintain day after day, year after year. Because who wants to witness this sort of scene:

HOMER SIMPSON: *What do you mean by "suggested donation"?*
MUSEUM CLERK: *Pay any amount you wish, sir.*
HOMER: *And uh, what if I wish to pay… zero?*
CLERK: *That is up to you.*
HOMER: *Ooh, so it's up to me, is it?*
CLERK: *Yes.*
HOMER: *I see. And you think that people are going to pay you $4.50 even though they don't have to? Just out of the goodness of their… Well, anything you say! Good luck, lady, you're gonna need it!*

So help keep the "free" in freedom and be a dear: make sure you exit through the gift shop. — (M)

ⓘ

ABOUT THE WRITER: Robert Bound is MONOCLE's Culture editor and wonders why people queue to pay for Madame Tussaud's when they could walk right into the National Gallery for free. Sure, you can't get your picture taken with a waxwork dictator but there are quite a few scary popes.

ESSAY 03
The scarlet workhorse
In praise of the Routemaster
——

The London bus is much more than a way of getting from A to B. From the original model that still runs in the centre of town to the sleek new-generation hybrid that glides far and wide, it is both an emblem of the city worldwide and a sight that says to travelling Londoners, 'Welcome home.'

by Alicia Kirby, Monocle

London's double-decker bus is an international icon and revered as a masterpiece of British design. Knitting together the fabric of the city, the Routemaster belongs in the pantheon of industrial greats alongside wide-bodied black cabs and red telephone boxes. For Londoners, the Routemaster is more than just a mode of transport: the vehicle is part of our civic identity and has the ability to tug at our collective heartstrings.

Conjuring up memories of carefree childhoods, rebellious teenage years and the struggles of our twenties and beyond, the Routemaster has always been with us. It was there when we tenderly held hands with a first love or illicitly smoked cigarettes on its top deck sheltered by the arches of its primrose-yellow ceiling (a colour chosen specifically for its capacity to disguise nicotine stains, the by-product of a time when smoking was allowed on public transport). Every Londoner has their own bus memory and their own bus story to tell; that tartan moquette livery has accommodated millions of people over the years who have loved, laughed and even given birth on its seats.

Every day these two-storey red billboards unapologetically meander at a snail's pace through the tangle of London's streets. In all a fleet of 8,700 buses serve more than 19,500 bus stops 24 hours a day, seven days a week, digesting and ejecting throngs of commuters.

Originally designed in 1954, the Routemaster hasn't always had an easy ride. In 2005 its future was in doubt when, aside from a single special heritage service on route 15, it was taken off the road and condemned to bus-garage limbo. Usurped by a growing fleet of bland and vulgar "bendy buses" that awkwardly navigated through city traffic, the Routemaster's planned extinction became a source of outrage as London mourned its loss. Tapping into a mood of nostalgia, British politician Boris Johnson used the buses as a political ticket to victory in his 2008 electoral campaign to become Mayor of London. Pledging to reinstate the Routemaster, vehicles that he declared the pulsing red arteries of the city, Johnson triumphed and the double-deckers began to trundle through the streets once again.

"Every Londoner has their own bus memory; the Routemaster's tartan moquette upholstery has accommodated millions of people over the years who have loved, laughed and even given birth on its seats"

Top bus routes
—
Route C2: From Kentish Town to Marylebone.
Route 9: From Hammersmith to Kensington Palace, the Royal Albert Hall and the Somerset House.
Route 24: From Camden Town to Victoria Station via Parliament Square and Westminster Abbey.

Johnson not only restored the Routemaster to its former glory but was also behind the call to have the original vehicle redesigned. A competition was held and in 2011 British designer Thomas Heatherwick came up with a contemporary iteration of the vehicle that had been part of the city's fabric for more than 60 years. Although some people worried that a big-name designer would tinker too much with the original concept, Heatherwick's New Routemaster was a triumph.

In its updated form the contemporary double-decker is an ode to past engineering excellence with an aesthetic that nods to a streamlined future. Built for purpose and currently operating on 11 routes (with more than 800 buses set to be in service by 2016), the diesel-electric hybrid is a more voluptuous version of its older sibling. It has restored the wondrous sense of occasion to the London bus ride that a snaking single-deck bendy bus could never recreate.

Heatherwick has been successful in capturing the dignity, formality and sense of wonder that always went hand in hand with riding a Routemaster. Londoners love their double-deckers and, luckily for us, it looks like they are here to stay for a while yet. — (M)

ABOUT THE WRITER: Alicia Kirby is a MONOCLE contributing editor. Having grown up in Tokyo, she now lives in London's Kentish Town and commutes to Midori House on the top deck of the C2, her favourite double-decker bus route.

ESSAY 04

Guts and glory
The City of London

What is now London's centre of finance was the square mile from which the entire city first sprung. Exploring it reveals everything you need to know about the character, construction and catastrophes that have since shaped the British capital.

*by Tom Morris,
Monocle*

Did you ever hear the one about Frederick Alfred Croft? He saved a lunatic woman from suicide at Woolwich Arsenal Station in 1878 but was then run over by a train. Chances are you haven't but if you have it's because you've visited one of my favourite places in London: Postman's Park, located in the City. In this green little quarter surrounded by office blocks sits a wall of modest plaques dedicated to Londoners who died trying to help others. Plucky civilians who drowned in the Thames after jumping in to save someone. Courageous souls who ran into fires to save strangers and themselves died in the flames.

It's an admittedly morbid but also very heartwarming place, and one of the many weird and wonderful memorials dotted around (the Animals in War structure on Park Lane, too: "They Had No Choice"). London has never been very good at highlighting its qualities but if you look at Postman's Park – and, more importantly, at other corners of the City of London, the capital's now financial heart – you'll see one of its most special traits shine crystal clear: its guts.

London was built in rings. Each era saw one spurt of development circle another around the City, pushing the metropolis further and further out. Starting somewhere in the centre, it vaguely went from Elizabethan to Georgian, from there to Victorian, Edwardian and then on to postwar suburbia on the outskirts of the city. The great thing about the old City is that it has been razed to the ground so many times, either by the Great Fire, World Wars or overzealous property developers.

"The great thing about the old City is that it has been razed to the ground so many times, either by the Great Fire, World Wars or overzealous property developers"

Favourite spots
—
01 **Paternoster Square, City**
The way the architecture
frames St Paul's is sublime.
02 **Finsbury Circus, City**
Perfectly grand, round
city square.
03 **St Botolph-without-
Bishopsgate Gardens, City**
Peaceful spot by Liverpool
Street Station.

There is no better place to understand London's character and history than within this microcosm. The very nature of London – tough, hardy, macho (I always think cities are gendered: Paris is definitely a woman, as are Kyoto and Stockholm; London, Helsinki, São Paulo, all men) – summed up in one square mile at its heart.

We could start at the London Wall, built by the Romans around Londinium, which is still visible in some parts of the City. But that was the Romans. For the Brits, the best place to start is London's first skyscraper: The Monument. It was completed in 1677 to commemorate the rebuilding of London after the Great Fire of 1666. That fire pulled almost the entire wooden city to the ground, with the exception of St Paul's Cathedral and Guildhall (both made of stone). This Doric column – made of Portland stone – marked a new wave of building for London. The Monument rises 61 metres, marking the distance between its base and where the

fire started at a bakery on Pudding Lane. Now The Monument looks a bit piddly because it is dwarfed by far grander edifices but climbing up to its peak (and you should), you still get a sense of the bravura that came about as London rebuilt itself after the flames that had ripped through it. It's still the world's tallest isolated stone column; London's gigantic middle finger to some baker that tried to fell it.

Now, a great fire wasn't the only thing that St Paul's survived. Almost 300 years later, huge swathes of the city were reduced to the ground once more, this time by German bombers. One of the most poignant symbols of the resilience of Londoners are the black-and-white photographs of Sir Christopher Wren's masterpiece during the Blitz. It's hard not to be stirred by the magnificence of this edifice shining bright among the rubble.

St Paul's is not a patch on St Peter's in Rome and lacks the high drama of Notre Dame in Paris or the ridiculous whimsy of the Sagrada Família in Barcelona. But as an emblem of a city's character there's nothing finer. For a start, Wren's take on classicism is as London as it gets: tempered, tasteful, a touch withdrawn. More to the point, nothing exemplifies the broad-shouldered hardiness of London better than this brutish survivor.

Though it endured great fires and wars, it's troubling that the one thing that has finally dampened the power of old Paul is something that shouldn't be a threat at all: architecture. Even those new to London will be aware of what's happened to its skyline in recent years. A whole cluster of weird and wonderful vegetables, kitchen instruments and communication devices – some eyesores, some landmarks – have taken over, all crowding around St Paul's yet not one a patch on it. But in the end that's what makes Londoners unique: their ability to adapt. To new cultures, trends, societies and, yes, architecture.

If you look back at the history of the built environment in this part of London, one thing is clear: what goes up will one day come down. Gherkins and cheese-graters will join 1960s office blocks and Elizabethan alleyways as a hodge-podge of relics. Layer upon layer of construction and destruction and, above all, progress.

It is little wonder that the emblem of the City of London is a dragon: in this part of London, even those that tried and failed get their own plaque. As we say in the UK, it's not the winning but the taking part that counts. — (M)

ABOUT THE WRITER: Tom Morris is MONOCLE's Design editor and also hosts *Section D*, Monocle 24's radio show on architecture and design. Tune in every Tuesday at 19.00 UK time.

ESSAY 05
Drink and be merry
~~Craft-beer revolution~~

The re-emergence of small breweries in the past decade is a good reason to seek out London's more thought-through pubs. Here enthusiastic and knowledgeable staff can introduce you to the beers weening city dwellers off fizzy lager and back to the real thing.

*by Pete Brown,
author*

London was once the most important brewing city in the world. Two of the greatest ever beer styles – porter and India pale ale (IPA) – were born here. In the late 19th century, London's pubs were the finest drinking establishments on Earth. Italian architects built the "gin palaces" that gave ordinary people a fleeting glimpse of the high life.

But in the 20th century, London lost its brewing mojo. Rising property values, falling sales and insane traffic meant that London's breweries closed, merged and moved out of town. Britain developed a taste for continental lager over pale ale. Porter was in effect extinct by the 1990s.

The low point came on 25 September 2006. That was the day that Young's – a

"The best are reinterpreting lost London beer styles from old brewing records and blending influences from the spicy Belgian farmhouse saison beers with British standards and American flair"

brewery in Wandsworth since 1576 – closed its doors. That left just two breweries in London: Fullers, which launched in 1845, and Meantime, which arrived in 2000.

I remember the day well because I was in Boulder, Colorado. This mountain town with a population of about 100,000 had 15 breweries at the time and I was trying to make my way around as many of them as I could. Back home, London – a city of eight million people – had just two. And forget Boulder; towns such as Sheffield, Derby and Nottingham put London to shame in terms of how many breweries they had and the range and quality of beers they produced.

But if there's one thing London hates it's being outclassed by any other city in anything at all. When the fightback came it was swift: in five years London reclaimed its position as arguably the world's most important beer city.

The global crash in 2008 changed the way a lot of Londoners thought about their priorities in life. It wasn't long before disillusioned desk dwellers began swapping suits for overalls and opening microbreweries. From two beer-makers in 2006 there were close to 25 by 2011. The London Brewers' Alliance, formed in 2010, says that by the end of 2014 there were about 60.

Originally in awe of the US craft-beer scene, these brewers all produce fragrantly fruity pale ales. But the best are transcending their influences, reinterpreting lost London beer styles from old brewing records, blending influences from Belgian farmhouse *saison* beers with British standards and American

Perfect pubs

01 Nags Head, Knightsbridge
Charming curio-crammed villagey affair.
02 The Lansdowne, Primrose Hill
Understated yet charming.
03 The Old Truman Brewery, Brick Lane
One of London's most historic brewing names.

flair to produce a broader range of flavours and styles than the capital has ever seen.

Breweries are springing up in all parts of London and the best way to taste across the whole city is to visit one of the new breed of craft-beer bars. The Draft House and Craft Beer Co each have outlets across the capital. The Rake in Borough Market, Dukes Brew & Que in Haggerston and the Euston Tap at Euston Station are similarly packed with a mind-boggling range of beers, with staff happily offering tasters to anyone struggling to choose.

Some commentators dismiss craft beer as a hipster fad that will last only as long as it takes for outrageous beards to become uncool. But both the craft-beer revolution and London's beer pedigree have deeper roots. The first of the new wave of London craft beers – real ales from Sambrook's, crisp pale ales from Meantime and perfect lagers from Camden Town – are increasingly common in regular, mainstream pubs and they are merely the vanguard.

To paraphrase the man who once described a London brewery as having the potential to make people "rich beyond the dreams of avarice": anyone who tires of London beer tires of life. — (M)

ABOUT THE WRITER: Pete Brown is a northerner who moved to London more than half a lifetime ago and has become an award-winning drinks writer. He still hasn't given up trying to educate southerners about the correct way to serve a pint of beer.

ESSAY 06

And the bands play on
Capital music venues

───

It can be a tough crowd but the populace of London has got used to being richly entertained over the centuries, a facet of the city that has left it awash with venues for music lovers. From gilded rock palaces to intimate jazz bars, we suggest a selection of spaces that hit just the right note.

*by Paul Noble,
Monocle 24*

What brings you to London? The architecture, the food, the shopping? For many it is the city's deep and varied musical heritage.

London's reputation as a hothouse of musical talent is on a par with Philadelphia, Detroit and New York. From Bowie to Blur, Kate Bush to Katy B, London's ability to spawn and nurture distinctive and influential artists is thanks in part to its diversity of music venues.

If you're after a true London one-off head to the Union Chapel in north London's Islington. This handsome church is still very much fulfilling its original purpose but at night it turns into one of the most enthralling music venues in London; the perfect venue for concerts that manage to feel intimate yet grand. A mix of extravagant styling, sympathetic acoustics and palpable religious undercurrents seem to add a touch of magic to any show there, with artists generally digging deep and reconfiguring their sets and line-ups to pay tribute to the extraordinary setting.

Soho's reputation as a place of sharp suits and overly posh soirées may have been dented in recent years by the influx of ambitious property developers but, if you look hard enough, traces of the old vibe still linger. For jazz lovers the iconic Ronnie Scott's is an unparalleled joy. Renovated in 2006, the main room with tiered seating, superb sound and world-class line-ups make this an essential stop for touring artists.

When it comes to the grand venues, London leads the way

Must-see music venues

───

01 Ronnie Scott's, Soho
The capital's best jazz joint.
02 606 Club, Chelsea
For the food and jazz combo.
03 Village Underground, Shoreditch
Hosts everything from live gigs to exhibitions and theatre.

with several magnificent converted music halls. Where once, in the century before last, an evening would usually feature any number of peculiarly British strains of "variety" acts – trained dogs, expert whistlers, soft-shoe shufflers – now the biggest names in rock and pop can be found. Hammersmith Apollo regularly has its name hijacked by sponsors but somehow still manages to create an intimate experience for thousands of people.

If you're after something a little grittier, Brixton Academy or the Kentish Town Forum both offer the scale and volume needed for a momentous communal experience. Meanwhile Camden's Roundhouse, once used as a turning station for steam trains, was repurposed as a music venue and hosted the acid-tinged wig-out HQ of the 1960s. It is now, finally, a stellar arts centre with live performance spaces, studios, a restaurant and arts hub, with profits from the shows feeding into projects that nurture the next generation of creative talent.

And what of the smaller venues? The Lexington in Islington is that rarest of beasts: a pub with genuinely great music in an intimate setting. If the band isn't doing it for you, simply chat to the barman about sampling one of the 100 bourbons on offer. Café Oto in Dalston has built a reputation for some of the most fearless and uncompromising contemporary music, from free jazz to experimental electronica; rewarding but not for the faint of heart. Club 606 is surely the most swinging place in Chelsea (an area that doesn't swing quite as hard as it once did).

Then we come to the jewel in the crown, perhaps the finest venue London has to offer: the Royal Albert Hall. No, it's not perfect acoustically – the giant mushrooms hanging from the ceiling won't be causing the Concertgebouw to lose any sleep – but in the sweet spot of scale and intimacy, and a dramatic setting which still allows the audience to focus on the music, it's one of the best in the world. Almost every artist who has performed there acknowledges the sense of achievement that comes with playing the most spectacular music space in London. — (M)

"London's ability to spawn and nurture distinctive and influential artists is in part down to the diversity of its music venues. Any visitor would be well advised to take advantage of the city's varied musical spots"

i

ABOUT THE WRITER: Paul Noble is a radio producer and a stalwart of Monocle 24. He's currently running his own members' club for music aficionados called Spiritland. Music was his first love and it will be his last.

Welcome. Now get lost
Strolling the hidden city

After the Great Fire of 1666 there was a proposal to rebuild London on a grid system. Thankfully for residents and visitors alike it was dropped (the plans were sold to Philadelphia instead) and the capital's streetmap remained a chaotic, intriguing invitation to the urban explorer.

*by David Michon,
Monocle 24*

Really heavy rain happens only rarely in London. Usually you're stuck with a kind of mist that's not quite wet enough to require you to open your umbrella. Rest assured though that if and when the clouds overhead do burst you won't be too far from a cosy pub to jump into, shake yourself off and wait out the deluge. A good excuse – not that one is ever needed here – for a mid-afternoon pint.

But not all pubs are created equal. The best in London are rarely the most obviously placed on the map. They're tucked away in residential side streets rather than main thoroughfares, or maybe even slap-bang in the middle of a park. The easiest way to hear of them is by word of mouth but the best way to discover them (if you're so lucky) is by chance, on a stroll.

Choosing to wander through London on foot can help unlock so much of what makes it unique, not just the better pubs. Here you'll find a city that was seemingly made to get lost in and that rewards you for allowing yourself to do just that. Physically the streets of London meander and as they do so they drift through the ages psychologically: they switch direction or name at a sometimes-alarming rate. A 2,000-year history has, inevitably, left us with a complicated arrangement; even after a third of London was wiped clean by the Great Fire of 1666, the medieval street plan mostly held its grip in the centre. It can seem chaotic, the logic of the pattern having long since become outdated or obscured. Narrow, twisting alleys can lead to dominating squares (or nowhere); titbits of curiosity can await. On a walk in the City I stumbled upon a bronze statue dedicated to Dr Samuel Johnson's cat Hodge. It put a smile on my face.

Often, too, there's more to London's streets than what lies at ground level. Of the 21 tributaries to the Thames that lie within Greater London, two thirds are partially or wholly underground, replaced at the surface by streets that follow their paths or carry their names. You can stroll down each one still, even down to the banks of the Thames to see the mere trickle those rivers and streams have become. It's an access point to a pre-urban place that many cities can't offer. (MONOCLE's very

> *"London can only rarely afford the visitor a neat route. Here one should ideally plan for a bit of time to saunter off the path, to be drawn by a glimpse of gothic spire or a flash of stately canal"*

Hidden gems

01 Parkland Walk, Highgate
London's longest-standing
nature reserve.
02 The Mayflower, Southwark
On Sundays the pub is
illuminated by candle light.
**03 Horniman Museum and
Gardens, Forest Hill**
Visit for the overstuffed
taxidermy walrus.

headquarters, Midori House, sits immediately above the buried Tyburn River. To trace it and others, pick up Tom Bolton's very excellent walking guide *London's Lost Rivers*.)

Other cities hold their secrets, of course. Milan's beauty is largely found in private courtyards; the best restaurants in Hong Kong are seven storeys up and minimally signed. London's secrets give much more intriguing hints, picked up simply by being on foot and found most enjoyably through that mythical creature of successful cities: serendipity. Stumbling across that quaint local pub at the first crack of thunder, for instance. Or finding yourself weaving down a cobbled-over stream trying to make your way to dinner.

An element of discovery and a sense of good fortune tend to produce a deep appreciation of the moment and an ownership of it. This is an important complement to ticking through the to-do's of a guidebook (even this one). What is most striking about London's streets as a visitor is that in many places their complexity prevents you from simply marching around. In New York or the modern parts of Barcelona you are carried along by the grid: pick a pace and count down the blocks until you get from A to B, perhaps with a stop in a shop or two. London can only rarely afford you a neat route. Here one should ideally plan for a bit of time to saunter off the path, to be drawn in by the glimpse of a bombed-out church or a flash of stately canal.

As Rebecca Solnit quotes in her book *A Field Guide to Getting Lost*: "How will you go about finding that thing the nature of which is totally unknown to you?" London has no single personality so it demands a more granular investigation. It is a megacity whose charm is found in its finest details and whose neighbourhoods can be schizophrenic, suddenly changing in demographic from one street to the next. A ramble is the best way to crack these codes. In a city with such a literally and figuratively layered history, whizzing through its arteries doesn't do it justice.

Cities are great places because of their texture, not their façades or function. London isn't a global capital simply because of Canary Wharf, more in spite of it. (Note: don't bother walking through Canary Wharf.) So lace up your runners and hit the pavement; choose your neighbourhood, start with coffee in hand and stop as often as you like. — (M)

ABOUT THE WRITER: David Michon is the producer of Monocle 24's *The Urbanist* and managing editor of Winkreative. After three successive tyre punctures, he has opted to punish his bicycle with a winter shackled to the railings and instead commutes to work for an hour by foot (perfect for catching up on podcasts).

ESSAY 08
Home from home
Our mixed-up metropolis

———

It doesn't matter if you are from Poland, Italy, Somalia, France, Germany or even Birmingham: if you live in London (and know how to use an escalator on the Underground) then you are officially a Londoner.

by Steve Bloomfield, Monocle

Along the soulless walk from aeroplane to immigration hall, Heathrow Airport does its best to welcome new arrivals. Large photos of stereotypical Londoners – the Beefeater, the pearly king, the cabbie – stare out at you, their arms open and grins fixed. The impact can be ruined somewhat if the first actual Londoner who greets you is a sour-faced border-control official. And then you're out and we start ripping you off with a train or cab that costs a small fortune.

The UK can feel like a country that doesn't feel comfortable with outsiders. Politicians talk about immigration as if it's something terrible while newspapers come up with new ways in which visitors to this island are ruining it for us Brits.

And yet here, in the nation's capital, things are different. This city with more immigrants than any other actually rather likes it. We don't vote for extremist parties, we celebrate the fact we've got more French people than Nantes and Bordeaux and we take full advantage of the most varied culinary scene in the world.

That's partly because London has always been a city of migrants. Not just from abroad but from the rest of the country, too. From Dick Whittington onwards we've gravitated towards London in a way that is rarely seen in other capitals. Unlike Italy there is no equivalent to Milan; London is the UK's media and fashion hub. Unlike Germany there is no equivalent to Frankfurt; London is the centre for finance.

For far too many professions, London is the only place to be. It sucks people out of villages, towns and cities across the UK, dragging us down here to moan about house prices and constantly remind people where we're really from but ultimately concede that actually, London is far better than home.

This could all make London a bloated, crowded, competitive city (and in some ways it is) but it also makes it vibrant and ever-changing. There are other cities around the world that can say the same but the main reason London succeeds is because its migrants quickly become its citizens. The city becomes our home in a way that rarely happens in other similarly multicultural cities around the world. We become Londoners first, Poles, Swedes or Brummies second. By and large we don't disappear to our enclaves; our neighbours are Somali on one side and Italian on the other.

Becoming a true citizen of London involves no tests about history, no mountain of paperwork, no requirement to earn a certain amount of money. If a test were to be invented, a question to ask to determine whether someone is a real Londoner, it would be difficult to come up with anything more effective than this: when you are travelling on the Underground, do you stand on the right-hand side of the escalator?

If you answer "Yes" then well done, you're a Londoner. There is nothing more life-affirming than watching someone stride up an escalator, say "Excuse me!" in a passive-aggressive manner then mutter to themselves in Portuguese as the tourist shuffles to the right.

How long will this continue, though? For too many of us, living here has become too expensive. House prices have soared; in some areas they rose by 50 per cent in 2014 alone. As people are pushed further out into the suburbs, existing communities find their areas changing. Some of those changes may be for the better but what does it matter that there

Happy hangouts

01 **Chatsworth Road, Clapton**
A street (and market) that hasn't lost sight of its roots.
02 **Victoria Park, Hackney**
We're spoilt for choice with green space in London.
03 **National Theatre, Southbank**
Home to some of the world's greatest theatre.

are now five independent coffee shops if your rent keeps going up? That leads to more upheaval, more people moving further out and communities breaking up. And where will they move? Will London just expand east, sucking up Essex? Will we all live in Zone 6? We're not building houses cheaply or quickly enough and the London dream is getting tougher.

Yet those new arrivals keep coming: from southern Europe and northern towns where jobs are scarce; from warzones and former colonies; from other capital cities around the world. London attracts us all because it's a truly global city where anyone can feel at home. And whatever its problems – and there are many – it will stay that way. It will stay that way because people like you will come here, you will stand on the right and you will become a Londoner. — (M)

i

ABOUT THE WRITER: Steve Bloomfield is MONOCLE's executive editor. He was born in Birmingham and moved to London in 2003. In the intervening years he has come to grudgingly accept that London is, on balance, slightly better than Birmingham.

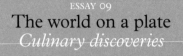

ESSAY 09

The world on a plate
Culinary discoveries

There are almost as many different cuisines on offer in London as there are languages to be heard on its streets. Whichever delicacy takes your fancy, there will be a spot somewhere in the city that serves a superlative example – and part of the pleasure for food lovers is in the seeking.

by Markus Hippi, Monocle 24

Why didn't all this happen earlier? Walking down streets where every restaurant you pass is better than the last, it is surprising to learn that, just two decades ago, London's food scene was a bit of an embarrassment. Today the capital has become a culinary destination that rarely disappoints. There is so much more to British cuisine than Sunday roast and fish and chips.

For me the excitement of daily culinary discoveries hasn't faded, despite having lived in London for a few years now. The city's restaurant scene is like the British Museum: there is so much to take in that the best approach is to return to it again and again. Take your time and choose a specific cuisine then allow yourself to savour its signature offerings.

I wouldn't say that my culinary adventures had a great start, though. When I first moved here from Helsinki in 2011 I was truly excited to be in this buzzing capital where nationalities and influences from around the world come together to create a unique environment. I would wake up in the morning and pick up a flat white from my local Australian café, continue with a light Asian lunch followed by something Mediterranean for dinner.

What I learned (the hard way) is that to enjoy this kind of routine indulgence and diversified menu you need to either choose the neighbourhood where you live wisely or be willing to spend a fair amount of time commuting across the city.

Imagine my not-so-pleasant surprise when I moved into a flat in north London only to discover that in this area my food options were limited to just two: either a kebab from one of the Turkish restaurants or groceries from a Polish corner shop. A similar pattern emerged when I moved to east London. All of a sudden Turkish and Polish cuisines became a distant memory as I was surrounded by restaurants serving south Asian food.

Finding the best food spots in London takes patience, local knowledge and luck. Sure, you can check out Michelin-star listings or various rankings online. But the smaller places you get to know and love don't inhabit such lists.

Nowadays I live in a corner of London that's renowned for a youthful and creative demographic. Once again the restaurants follow a certain pattern: for some reason there is no escaping avocado here. It's

"Finding the best food spots in London takes patience, local knowledge – and luck. You can check out Michelin-star rankings but the smaller places you get to know and love don't inhabit such lists"

Top foodie spots

01 The Bull & Last, Highgate
Amazing food and location:
opposite Hampstead Heath.
02 E Mono, Kentish Town
Probably the best kebab
shop in London.
**03 Parliament Hill
Farmers' Market**
For the gourmet macarons.

everywhere: in salads, omelettes and pies.
It is even on toast.

Sometimes when I think that London
is trying too hard with its food crazes,
I remind myself of what my home city
Helsinki has to offer. Avocado, for
example, has never appeared on any slice
of toast. And how about those global
influences? I definitely prefer what's
on the menu in London.

And although I don't understand
the fish-and-chips obsession I really
enjoy the other traditional British food
offerings – and I encourage you to try
them, too. It's hard to beat a good Sunday
roast (although the airy Yorkshire pudding
is a bit pointless). Another reason to
love the food offerings of this city is
the availability of good Jewish fare; I
love the rye bread salt-beef sandwich at
Reubens in Marylebone. And check out
Brick Lane's bagel bakeries, where the
combination of cream cheese and salmon
on offer resonates with my Nordic genes.

And speaking of cheese, I must admit
that I have developed a love affair with
British dairy produce. In fact, I could
probably live solely on cheddar for the
rest of my life. — (M)

ABOUT THE WRITER: Markus Hippi is a producer and
presenter of *The Menu*, Monocle 24 radio's weekly
food-and-drink show. He's from Finland so bright
Nordic nights are close to his heart; however, he has
decided not to move back to Helsinki until the city
has as many great Asian restaurants as London.

ESSAY 10
London love
City of seduction

This place won't ever
beg for your adoration;
it's just not that kind of
town. But if you stick
around long enough and
occasionally give it your
undivided attention, the
city will eventually reveal
what all the fuss is about.
Trust us, it's worth
the wait.

*by Andrew Tuck,
Monocle*

I think I'm in love. This is the line
that people who move to this city
wait to hear dropping from their
own lips. But sometimes the
dating game goes on too long and
the possibility of love slips away.
Sometimes people just get too
many rejections and move on to a
new potential partner. And let's be
honest, as date mates go this one
can be annoying, haughty, stone-
faced, confusing and not quite
as hygienic as you might expect
from a would-be life partner. Yet
people do fall in love with this

mighty metropolis, this tough old cookie, this temperamental marvel – London.

You may have realised by now (especially if you are reading this essay sat in a London café on a steel-grey day to dodge the rain) that our capital lacks the frilly charm of Paris or the jaw-dropping classicism of Rome. Or reliable weather. It's a city of humble red bricks and slabs of Portland stone that can seem small-minded or austere. It's also a city where you often feel penned in: you have to head to Hampstead Heath or Primrose Hill before you get a good view and some clean breeze.

But perhaps it's because of all the defences and impediments that London puts in your way that, when love does strike, it feels special. Yes, there are times when this town takes you by surprise and you know that you are hooked.

It's when you are in Regent's Park on a frosty morning walking the perimeter of London Zoo and a shaggy-coated camel glances at you over the fence and there is nobody else around.

It's in the spring when you go down to Columbia Road Flower Market on a Sunday. You push through the crowd, all armed with daffodils and tulips, and the stallholders are shouting out their bargains; you feel the pulse of an older London.

It's when you cross the River Thames in a taxi at dusk and the view down to the Houses of Parliament is a purple haze and the Thames drifts on in its magisterial silence.

It's walking into the Turbine Hall at Tate Modern surrounded by people from all over the world, milling and eddying in a modern town square, and you feel at the heart of the world.

It's seeing Turner's painting of "The Fighting Temeraire" in the National Gallery, which shows a ship from the Battle of Trafalgar being towed away to be scrapped. It's perhaps the most famous and glorious picture in all England.

It's the tiniest detail that could so easily be missed. How about the plaque in Queen Square that marks where a zeppelin dropped its bombs during the First World War?

It's the postwar concrete architecture that's the best in the world. Kiss the ground in front of the National Theatre and offer thanks to Sir Denys Lasdun!

It's coffee in Shoreditch. It's dinner at The Delaunay when you stay and stay.

It's the sun. When it strikes that red brick and cool stone you see a

Bloomsbury favourites
———
01 Lincoln's Inn Fields
All but silent for Sunday strolls.
02 Coram's Fields
Vast playground where adults can only enter if accompanied by children.
03 Russell Square
The archetypal London square.

"Perhaps it's because of all the impediments that London puts in your way that, when love does strike, it feels very special. Yes, there are times when this town takes you by surprise and you know you are hooked"

beauty emerge from the shadows.

It's about community and anonymity. Here you can be who you want to be. To hell with small-town England!

It's knowing that you are one of millions who over time have taken to this stage.

It's a city that reveals itself like a very slow stripper. A tease.

This guide book acts as a fine introduction and takes you to places where this love may take hold. But you need to get out there, start wandering and wondering. Go to the best clubs; hit the bars; drink and be drunk; eat and consume. But just get out there.

And then it will happen.

You'll have just come across Postman's Park in the City of London with its memorial to heroic self-sacrifice, or perhaps be getting back to your hotel at five in the morning when the streets are all empty, and you'll say to yourself, "You know what, I think I'm in love." — (M)

ⓘ
ABOUT THE WRITER: Andrew Tuck is MONOCLE's editor and the presenter of various Monocle 24 shows, including *The Urbanist*, the show about the cities we live in. Tune in at *monocle.com* to hear tales from the city – including London, of course.

ESSAY 11

Crafting the city
The art of making
———

An exploration of London's streets will reveal the capital as a city of artisans. From heritage brands to niche antiques, there's plenty to be found in settings that far surpass everyday retail environments.

by Hugo Macdonald, Studioilse brand director

"Did you know this cutlery was made by the same man who designed the traffic light?" I was a bright-eyed boy having tea with a teacher of mine and this was my first conscious understanding of design. It seemed preposterous that the same mind and hands were capable of conceiving a fork and a traffic light. David Mellor was the designer and I was transfixed.

Soon after, I visited Mellor's shop just off Sloane Square in west London. I was disappointed not to find traffic lights for sale but my gloom evaporated when the sales assistant took me on a journey through some of the many

"When people ask me to recommend retail places in London I list places where I know the contents can be brought to life by the people who work there"

different types of cutlery on show. Everything had a story. Everything was there for a reason and looked a certain way because it performed a special function. Who knew cutlery could be so clever?

There's been much moaning since the crash that there's little room in London for retail between big-brand showrooms, high-street hovels and rather "meh" museum shops. What tosh. The streets are packed with shops that are filled with stories about fascinating things as long as you know where to look.

Thanks to the accessibility provided by the web, everything is available everywhere nowadays. But a dusty old shop that smells of centuries past, staffed by an eager expert armed with encyclopaedic knowledge, is not something you buy through PayPal. When people ask me to recommend retail places in London I put together a list of strange destinations, big and small, old and new, where I know the contents can be brought to life by the people who work there.

After David Mellor, Alfie's Antiques Market in Marylebone is a safe bet. It's a quintessential London experience meandering round the 70-odd (and they certainly are odd) antiques dealers under one roof. You may not come to buy an art deco fireplace but you will leave with a head full of stories, the likes of which cannot easily be purchased. The dealers here love to talk and to share their tales and knowledge. The V&A is a more formal setting with ordered contents neatly categorised but Alfie's is definitely more fun.

After cutlery and antiques I advise a dose of contemporary design philosophy lest people think London only does old things. Jasper Morrison's shop is a hidden treat and portal to the inner thinking of London's greatest living industrial designer. You enter through a door marked 24B on Kingsland Road, down a short passageway and into his modest little shop. It is stocked with unremarkable but brilliant, helpful everyday tools – dishwasher racks, staplers, jugs, alarm clocks, trays and so on – some designed by Morrison, the majority collected over a life of travel and use. What links them

Design classics
—
01 Sir John Soane's Dulwich Picture Gallery
A surprising experience of space and light (and art).
02 Balfron Tower, Poplar
A lesser-known modernist gem.
03 St-George-in-the-East, Shadwell
Smaller than St Pauls but just as striking.

is their simple, perfect function. Or Super Normal as Morrison calls it. Buy his book of the same title while you're there and it will change the way you look at "things".

From Morrison to Mayfair, The New Craftsmen is a shop that brings old and new together; traditional skills with modern ideas. Founded by a trio of experienced retailers (including Mark Henderson, chairman of Gieves & Hawkes), the mission is to promote the craft and craftsmanship still alive in the British Isles and to dispel the myth that it's dying. The beautiful spot is a commissioning programme and retail platform for almost every native skill you care to imagine. Mohair blankets, woven willow trugs, gold-plated scissors and terracotta vessels with leather handles: they're all here. The mind boggles at the stories and skills but it's beautiful and fascinating and proof that, though many of the bigger industries might have dwindled, the knowledge of how to make things lives on in the UK.

Two essential revival brands to take in before you head home are Grenson and Sunspel to stock up on leather shoes and cotton basics respectively. The stories here are similar and familiar. They were both founded around the mid-19th century. Business boomed then declined with the waning of UK industry. But happily both

have been rescued from history in the last decade, attracting a new audience that cares about quality and provenance. Though the product speaks for itself, the London stores are perfect nuggets of contemporary retail that elevate the experience of shoe and T-shirt shopping to something more special. You might not want to "feel" history when you're buying underwear but trust me, it's better than it sounds.

Of course a lot of shopping requires extra luggage and I advise investing in a tidy Globe-Trotter to transport your stories home. The vulcanised fibreboard the company patented for its cases in 1901 is light, strong and durable; Edmund Hillary climbed Everest with them. It should get your David Mellor cutlery home just fine. — (M)

ABOUT THE WRITER: A former design editor at MONOCLE, Hugo Macdonald is now brand director of Studioilse. He has lived in 10 different flats (and one boat) around London for the past 15 years; his knowledge of local pubs spans the length and breadth of the entire city.

ESSAY 12

Capital letters
Design inspiration

——

If you keep your eyes open, fascinating fonts and tantalising typography can be spotted throughout London's streets. For the committed there are even some prime examples to be found in the city's cemeteries.

by Richard Spencer Powell, Monocle

Over the years I've often been asked what has been the biggest influence on the design of MONOCLE. Most people might expect a list of designers, studios, cinematographers or art movements. The actual answer is a street in London. Jermyn Street to be precise, just off Piccadilly. To my eye this road, made famous by its troupe of shirt-making proprietors, has more beautiful typography per metre than any other.

The black and gold of MONOCLE's brand identity are directly influenced by this decorative darling from London's Victorian era. Hand-painted gold-letter signage adorns nearly every storefront. From shirtmaker Harvie & Hudson to cheesemonger Paxton & Whitfield and the rear windows of Fortnum & Mason, smart serifs never appeared so charming.

Before moving to London I studied typography. Like most designers I began building a library of books, graphic

"Designers need ideas and this is one of the reasons why so many of them move to the capital"

design, architecture, photography and fashion periodicals – anything to sate my visual appetite. An early favourite in the beginnings of this collection was a study of the work of typographer Anthony Froshaug, who held a post at the city's Royal College of Art in the 1960s.

Reading this tome I discovered that Froshaug's headstone at Highgate Cemetery was made by another famous typographer: Eric Gill. Gill had assisted in making London Underground's typeface before moving on to create his own font, Gill Sans. This became the closest thing to a house font for the UK and is still seen on the BBC and every item of "Keep Calm and Carry On" merchandise.

I decided I needed to find the grave and this hallowed headstone so I headed up to the hills of north London. Although small, Highgate Cemetery is packed with a curious collection of émigrés from all over. And after an enjoyable hour searching around, I found the diminutive black tombstone. A name and a date were crisply etched into a black face, small but perfectly formed. It perhaps wasn't worth the trip but an occasional obsession can be a healthy thing.

I have read that you can find inspiration in everything and should look again if you can't. Designers need ideas and this is one of the reasons why so many of them move to the capital. London's 20,000 streets under the sky have never failed to inspire me; typographically, this most historic of European capitals has a full set of characters. — (M)

ABOUT THE WRITER: Richard Spencer Powell is MONOCLE's creative director. When he's not wandering around cemeteries looking for typefaces he can be found scouring stationery shops for them instead.

Culture
—— Arts guide

It's time to start the music; it's time to light the lights. Unless you're in a museum, of course. This is the bit that London's best at. Better at, in fact, than anywhere else in the world. People call it London's "cultural offering"; well, it is and it isn't. Quite a bit of the best stuff is free – the masterpieces and the magnificent museums in which you'll find them – but some of the rest of it needs to be sought out; not sleuthed after but located. When it comes to galleries and venues, London doesn't hide its light under a bushel. But that's almost the problem: there's *so much* of the stuff that you might be led up the wrong path, albeit a spangly one.

That's where this section of the book comes in: to keep you on the straight and narrow, to keep you from the sirens calling coquettishly from the jagged rocks. Here you go: the keys to the best rooms in the kingdom.

Picture perfect
——
A fifth of UK cinema screens are in London

Cinemas
Take a seat

①
Screen on the Green, Islington
Upper Street institution

Set among Upper Street's ever-changing cast of boutique stores and neighbourhood restaurants, this mainstay of the Everyman cinema chain has been serving up a well-selected blend of beyond-the-mainstream films since 1913. With its striking neon façade an Islington landmark, this purpose-built, single-screened, barrel-vaulted institution was recently revamped with a bar and deluxe seating.

Beyond the films it also hosts talks, Q&As, Saturday matinées, comedy nights and film events – including an Islington leg of the London Film Festival – making it an essential part of the capital's cinema landscape.
83 Upper Street, N1 0NP
+ 44 (0)871 906 9060
everymancinema.com

②
Rio, Hackney
Dalston indie

On-the-money film roster? Check. Art deco grandesse? Check. Artisan snacks? Check. Another neighbourhood cinema with a friendly yet cineaste feel, the heritage-protected Rio Cinema in Dalston is a popular venue with a vibrant buzz. The bar serves homemade cakes, organic sodas and freshly brewed Monmouth coffee as well as beers and wines to complement the films on offer. Plus, with the capital's best Turkish restaurants and late-night dive bars on the doorstep, you can turn a trip to the flicks into a big night out.
107 Kingsland High Street, E8 2PB
+ 44 (0)20 7241 9410
riocinema.org.uk

③
Firmdale Hotel Film Club, Central
Cinematic indulgence

Firmdale, the high-end hotel chain, holds weekly Film Clubs at three of its central London outposts – Covent Garden, Soho and Charlotte Street – that give guests and in-the-know filmgoers the chance to drop in and take advantage of the lunch, dinner or afternoon-tea menu before the film begins. With film choices spanning classic to contemporary in state-of-the-art screening rooms accompanied by champagne and a set menu, this is an oh-so-civilised affair guaranteed to impress your film partner.
At various locations
firmdalehotels.com

④
Curzon Mayfair, Mayfair
Arthouse original

Curzon's Mayfair base has been an arthouse institution since 1934 and was one of the first British venues to show foreign-language films. Luxe carpets, Pullman seats and four-seater "royal boxes" add occasion to its two screening rooms; a venue has also opened in Bloomsbury.
38 Curzon Street, W1J 7TY
+ 44 (0)330 500 1331
curzoncinemas.com

'Lassie Come Home' is a cult classic

⑤
Electric Cinema, Notting Hill
Blanket coverage

Comfy leather armchairs come as standard in west London's most decadent screening room that – with its plush fixtures and fittings – channels a slice of old Hollywood glamour. Now more than a century old, the Electric's double beds, cashmere blankets and beer and wine list are all designed to enhance and elevate your cinematic experience. A sister venue has opened on Shoreditch's Redchurch Street but for a cinematic respite from the chatter of the Notting Hill set, the original Electric can't be beaten.
191 Portobello Road, W11 2ED
+ 44 (0)20 7908 9696
electriccinema.co.uk

London on film

01 Blow-Up, 1966: Life through the lens of a 1960s fashion photographer, arthouse staple *Blow-Up* captures the thrills and spills of Swinging London in its counter-cultural heyday.

02 The World is Not Enough, 1999: Although not James Bond's finest hour, one character does stand out. As an early high-octane River Thames boat chase takes place, the camera-panning, vertigo-inducing shots of the city via the Houses of Parliament, Tower Bridge and St Katharine Docks mean London never looked so exciting.

03 The Look of Love, 2013: Steve Coogan's take on the life of property and porn baron Paul Raymond paints a vivid picture of the 1960s sleaze and seduction that made his Soho neighbourhood such a hotspot both then and now.

Museums
Must-see collections

① British Museum, Bloomsbury
Classic colossus

Of course you're going to go to the British Museum and you have Sir Hans Sloane to thank, an avid collector who gifted his collection of 71,000 artefacts to King George II and thus brought about the foundation of the world's first national public museum.

Since its establishment in 1753, the museum has claimed some of the world's greatest "finds", from the Rosetta Stone to sculptures from the 2,500 year-old Athenian Parthenon temple. Take tea in Norman Foster's Great Court: a spectacular glass-roof dome that transformed the inner courtyard into the largest covered public square in Europe. A posh porch.
Great Russell Street, WC1B 3DG
+ 44 (0)20 7323 8299
britishmuseum.org

No jokes about me being 'armless, thank you

② Horniman Museum and Gardens, Forest Hill
Zone 3 delight

Maybe because of its location in Forest Hill, past the comfort of Zones 1 and 2, the Horniman is too often overlooked in museum hit lists. Founded in 1901 by tea trader and collector extraordinaire Frederick John Horniman, the museum is a treasure chest of wonderful oddities featuring eerie masks, voodoo objects and all kind of artefacts picked up during Horniman's travels. The 6.5-hectare landscaped gardens and ornate white conservatory make for a perfect Sunday afternoon escape.
100 London Road, SE23 3PQ
+ 44 (0)20 8699 1872
horniman.ac.uk

③
The V&A, South Kensington
The grand collection

Through the towering limestone
entrance of the Victoria and
Albert Museum (V&A) sits a
catalogued oasis of over 5,000
years of art and design. For the
traditionalists there are ceiling-
to-floor rooms of Victorian-era
collectibles, western European
sculptures dating back to the 4th
century and textiles from Middle
Ages British embroidery to Edo-
period Japanese kimonos.

But the collections aren't all
from bygone eras. If something
more modern appeals, make a
beeline for Room 106 to see a little
on the history of stage make-up
in the form of Kylie Minogue's
dressing room or visit the expansive
art deco display. Whichever era you
choose to explore, ensure you exit
through the gift shop: it is arguably
one of the best in London.
Cromwell Road, SW7 2RL.
+ 44 (0)20 7942 2000
vam.ac.uk

> **Vast collection**
> ——
> The museum
> contains at
> least 8 million
> objects

I might just have found inspiration for my next still life

(4)
Tate, Millbank & Bankside
Masterpieces

The Tate collection was first displayed in Sidney Smith's grand gallery at Millbank in 1897; now it's called Tate Britain, replete with its Constables and Turners. The collection has since grown to over 70,000 works dating back to 1500 by 3,000 UK and international artists.

In the new millennium, the contemporary portion of the collection was moved into the former Bankside power station redesigned by Herzog & de Meuron. Alongside expertly hosted pop-up exhibitions, the Tate Modern showcases artists including Picasso, Rothko, Matisse and Kandinsky and offers the best views of St Paul's.
*Tate Britain, Millbank, SW1P 4RG;
Tate Modern, Bankside, SE1 9TG
+44 (0)20 7887 8888
tate.org.uk*

TATE MODERN FACTS
01 The chimney of the power station is 99 metres tall, deliberately shorter than the dome of St Paul's Cathedral across the Thames.
02 Sir Giles Gilbert Scott, the architect of Bankside power station, was also the designer of the British red telephone box.
03 The third-floor espresso bar features two riverside balconies with stunning views.

(1)
The Wallace Collection, Marylebone
Fine-art treasure trove

Get a whiff of aristocratic Europe at the palatial 18th century Manchester House, former home of the Marquesses of Hertford. On display in the 25 galleries are art treasures collected by the family between 1760 and 1880. Expect to see masterpieces such as "The Laughing Cavalier" (1624) by Dutch master Frans Hals and François Boucher's "Madame de Pompadour" (1759) amid Rococo furniture. The vitreous courtyard houses the mostly worthwhile Peyton and Byrne brasserie.
*Hertford House, Manchester Square, W1U 3BN
+44 (0)20 7563 9500
wallacecollection.org*

(2) Hayward Gallery, Southbank
Brutalist charmer

Slightly hidden behind the entrance to the Royal Festival Hall, the Hayward Gallery is safely sheltered from the hordes strolling on the busy riverside. The Southbank Centre's most innovative venue prides itself on its in-the-know programmes: contemporary-art shows range from wide, thematic sweeps to solo exhibits from the likes of Antony Gormley, Tracey Emin and Martin Creed.

Inside and out, the Hayward Gallery is a brutalist cement cast but its huge, versatile spaces are put to the best use by ambitious installation work in ample, complex and multilevel exhibitions. Don't forget to peek at the outdoor platforms where some surprise alfresco piece always awaits, with the chaos of London as a fitting backdrop.
*Belvedere Road, SE1 8XX
+ 44 (0)20 7960 4200
southbankcentre.co.uk*

(3) Serpentine Gallery, Hyde Park
Garden delights

Having taken the name of the body of water in the middle of Hyde Park, the Serpentine Gallery also benefits from its pastoral surroundings. Set in the midst of Kensington Gardens, the Serpentine comprises two venues linked by a bridge over the lake. The original 1970s space (housed in a former tea pavilion built in the early 1930s) is worth a visit for its way with contemporary (and now modern) art: Moore, Kapoor, Basquiat, Hirst and Abramovic have all shown.

If the lavish landscape and great art is not enough of a draw, have a browse in the attached Koenig bookshop. Just around the corner at the Serpentine Sackler Gallery, a 2013 redesign by Zaha Hadid, you can get lost in interactive art installations before a bite at the gallery's glass-walled café.
*Kensington Gardens, W2 3XA
+ 44 (0)20 7402 6075
serpentinegalleries.org*

If I stare at this for long enough I might look clever

(4)

Whitechapel Gallery,
Whitechapel
Brick Lane trendsetter

Bringing art to the East End for over
a century is not the only headline
act that the trailblazing Whitechapel
Gallery can lay claim to. With Iwona
Blazwick as gallery director since
2001, the contemporary-art house
has taken risks and redefined the
niche of public galleries.

Giving Damien Hirst his first
solo show at a public-art gallery
(at London's ICA) is among one of
Blazwick's notable accomplishments
while at the helm, along with
her vision to extend the gallery's
boundaries to develop education
resources through workshops and
industry links for budding artists.
An expansion in 2009 has made the
trip to the bottom of Brick Lane
even more worthwhile, with greats
such as Pablo Picasso, Frida Kahlo
and English sculptor Mike Nelson
all having featured at different
points throughout the gallery's
extensive history.
77-82 Whitechapel High Street,
E1 7QX
+44 (0)20 7522 7888
whitechapelgallery.org

Commercial galleries
The art heart

① Victoria Miro, Islington
Cork Street mover

The movements of art dealer Victoria Miro's gallery describe the arcs in which London's art world has moved over the past 30 years: Cork Street to the east back to Mayfair again. In fact, that's a disservice to Miro's space in a converted furniture factory between Angel and Old Street – the heart of her wonderful enterprise. Miro's taste is always spot on, too: Grayson Perry, Idris Khan, Elmgreen & Dragset and Doug Aitken are all represented and shown with imagination (and a lot of space) on Wharf Road.
16 Wharf Road, N1 7RW
+44 (0)20 7336 8109
victoria-miro.com

❷ Lisson Gallery, Marylebone
Blazing a trail

Nicholas Logsdail was the earliest adopter of them all, opening his place (now places) on still-uncool Bell Street in 1967. A succession of landmark shows by artists – mainly sculptors in those days, who played a key role in changing contemporary art – proved that art had its place away from Cork Street. Richard Long, Sol LeWitt, Anish Kapoor and Tony Cragg have all since passed through and Lisson is now an international fixture at art fairs, too. But these spots off the Edgware Road are vital to London's beating art heart.
27 and 52 Bell Street, NW1 5DA
+44 (0)20 7724 2739
lissongallery.com

③ White Cube, Bermondsey
Art outside the box

Having moved from its former heartland on Hoxton Square near Shoreditch High Street, White Cube is now in St James's and Bermondsey – and it's the latter that is the biggest, boldest commercial space in London. What a hangar of delights Jay Jopling and his crew have assembled since its opening in 2011: important shows by Christian Marclay, Tracey Emin and Antony Gormley. The White Cube is always smart and never smarmy – though perhaps ever so slightly chilly.
144-152 Bermondsey Street, SE1 3TQ
+44 (0)20 7930 5373
whitecube.com

④ Michael Hoppen, Chelsea
Picture-perfect gallery

Michael Hoppen runs the best gallery for photography in London and a random visit to his space in Chelsea tends to be the equal of any museum visit for the same purpose. Hoppen was an editorial and commercial photographer who became a collector and then de facto dealer in 1993. Hoppen and his team are hands on with their artists and this small-gallery ethos ensures an environment that encourages questions, enquiry and anecdotes rather than an atmosphere overseen by icy gallerinas.
3 Jubilee Place, SW3 3TD
+44 (0)20 7352 3649
michaelhoppengallery.com

⑤ Marian Goodman, Soho
New York cool

The New York dealer's London space is a marvel of light, height and scale. Opening during 2014's Frieze week with a show by Richter, Goodman's roster of artists is formidable, their staging imaginative. A museum challenger.
5-8 Lower John Street, W1F 9DY
+44 (0)20 7099 0088
mariangoodman.com

⑥ Robilant + Voena, Mayfair
Renaissance men

This fine space on Dover Street is an antidote to any contemporary-enduced headache. Although it bills itself as a home to artists from the 15th to 21st century, the gallery's strength is in gorgeous oils by late renaissance Italians.
38 Dover Street, W1S 4NL
+44 (0)20 7409 1540
robilantvoena.com

Work of art

The members-only Chelsea Arts Club on Old Church Street has a rightfully louche history, a wonderful bar, a billiards table and plenty of paintings by august members and those that are bona fide artists. This is a lunching and drinking place – wear a scarf.

⑦

Stephen Friedman Gallery,
Mayfair
World view

Montréal-born Stephen Friedman
bought his first artwork at the
age of 13. At 31 he opened his
eponymous gallery in London's
West End, a stone's throw from
the clusters of art ventures on
Cork Street and Savile Row's
tailors. Today Friedman occupies
two neighbouring spaces on Old
Burlington Street as well as an
additional exhibition outpost across
the road.

Friedman has an international
portfolio made up of about 30
established contemporary artists,
including Yinka Shonibare, David
Shrigley, Thomas Hirschhorn,
Yoshitomo Nara and Catherine
Opie. "I'm all about longevity," he
says. "Tastes evolve quickly so the
idea is to tone the heat down a little
and maintain it over a long period
of time."
25-28 Old Burlington Street, W1S 3AN
+ 44 (0)20 7494 1434
stephenfriedman.com

No frills
——
Oto's simple
decor gives it
an intimate
vibe

Music venues
Listen live

Road to rhythm
——
London has a bewilderingly
rich musical make-up but you
don't always need a ticket to
experience it. During summer
months some of the best
sounds are on the streets: from
Caribbean rhythms at Notting
Hill to south London's Latin-
themed Carnaval
del Pueblo.

①

Café Oto, Dalston
Leftfield mainstay

For all the talk of London's "great"
venues, let's be honest: it would
be much cooler to see world-
renowned talent in your own or
a well-connected friend's front
room. Café Oto in Dalston is
that room. Its low-slung ceiling
and eschewing of conventional
performance norms such as a
stage or green room (hospitality
packages at the O2 are *that* way, my
friend) lend a cosy and unfussy feel
to a venue pushing unconventional,
sometimes challenging but never
unengaging line-ups.

Expect to see neighbourhood
noisemonger and Oto-regular
Thurston Moore sharing bills
with avant-jazzers such as Mats
Gustafsson. Or perhaps more
subdued acoustic sets from the
likes of rising Philadelphia folk
artist Steve Gunn playing with the
unsung London legend that is Mike
Cooper – a guitarist who turned
down the Rolling Stones. Told you
they're a picky bunch at Oto.
18-22 Ashwin Street E8 3DL
+ 44 (0)20 7923 1231
cafeoto.co.uk

(2) Roundhouse, Camden
On the right track

Some 150 years ago, Camden Roundhouse was a Victorian engineering marvel built to house railway engines, its once-revolving floor – essentially a fancy way to park trains – lending the building its shape. Later this cavernous north London monolith housed a gin distillery before becoming something of a speakeasy-cum-arts hangout during the 1960s and 1970s, reverberating to the sound of everyone from the Ramones to the Royal Exchange Theatre. Having sat empty and unloved during the 1980s, today a post-millennial rebirth means it rightfully reclaims its place as one of London's best state-of-the-art venues for up to 3,000 fans.

It is equally adept at delivering the "sonic holocaust" of My Bloody Valentine as it is the Mercury Prize's awards show. For Camden – that slightly shabby uncle of London neighbourhoods (the one who used to be in a band) – it's also something of an unofficial icon; it just took a century for anyone to realise. What goes around comes around.
Chalk Farm Road, NW1 8EH
+44 (0)30 0678 9222
roundhouse.org.uk

(3) Cecil Sharp House, Camden
Folk society

If you can call the vast expanse of Regent's Park a village green then we'll call Camden's Cecil Sharp House (just off the park's northeast corner) the village hall of the nation. It's where folk music, craft and all that's quaint can be stumbled upon during a lazy Saturday afternoon's wander.

Here you can learn anything from how to play a fiddle to clog dancing, or enjoy an evening of music from one of the venue's regular visiting musicians. And it's not all about the English, either: you're just as likely to see a talk with US alt-rock hero Kim Gordon or fall over trying to perfect an Argentinean tango at Cecil Sharp House as you are to encounter any wistful notion of country life. That's what the countryside is for.
2 Regent's Park Road, NW1 7AY
+44 (0)20 7485 2206
cecilsharphouse.org

Let's see you play 'Chopsticks' with talons

(4) The 606 Club, Chelsea
All that jazz

The 606 Club occupies a sedate corner of Chelsea that's a little more becoming of a crowd for whom a night of sublime jazz, Latin or R&B is as important as bagging a good table and a well-selected menu. Since 1976, the 606 has offered live music seven nights a week that focuses on British talent. Booking is advisable: due to licensing restrictions, non-members can only buy alcohol with a meal. There's no entrance fee but a music charge (around £10) will be added to the evening's bill, all of which goes to the band.
90 Lots Road, SW10 0QD
+44 (0)20 7352 5953
606club.co.uk

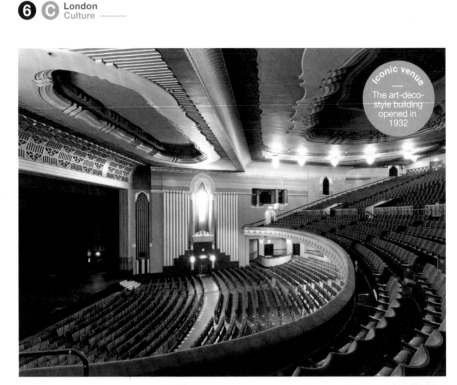

Iconic venue
──
The art-deco-style building opened in 1932

⑤

Eventim Apollo, Hammersmith
Interior marvel

Such is the lure of the art deco Hammersmith Apollo (now the Eventim thanks to sponsorship), artists from Kate Bush to Kings of Leon have chosen it as the location for documenting that hit'n'miss concept: the live record. But you can't blame bands for being seduced by its restored interiors, shined up to their 1930s glory by Foster Wilson in 2013. The venue now has enough sparkle to have tempted back one of its most celebrated performers: the aforementioned Bush, who returned for 22 concerts in 2014.
45 Queen Caroline Street, W6 9QH
+ 44 (0)20 8563 3800
eventimapollo.com

Catching a live show in London is a sound decision

Best of the rest
London media round-up

Radio: essential listening

01 **Danny Baker:** The Deptford native has been the wittiest, most whimsical and fearlessly creative voice on UK and London radio since the early 1980s. The former *NME* journalist's on-air style is university-of-life cum laude with encyclopaedic lashings of light-entertainment lore. In his current slot, Baker's show is dominated by themes to which callers offer anecdotes: "Trouble with a strap", "Then it started to get dark", etc. The Sausage Sandwich Game is the finest piece of quasi-quiz show nonsense on any medium.
The Danny Baker Show, BBC Radio 5 Live

02 **Matthew Sweet:** Sweet is a bit of a fount of knowledge on everything from what theatres did during the war to film, literature, comment pieces and general head-first cultural pluckiness. While the keen-eared will hear that Sweet's no London native, his eager intellect makes it clear why this town adopted him with open schedules.
Night Waves, BBC Radio 3

03 **In Our Time:** The most life-affirming renaissance man of strands on British radio is this series of discussions chaired by cultural kingpin Melvyn Bragg. Topics of dizzying scope and variety feature: Zen, the destruction of Carthage, Truth, The Corn Laws and Simone Weil, to name a few.
In Our Time, BBC Radio 4

Monocle 24

To break the hegemony of the BBC's radio output, give Monocle's own station a spin for culture, urbanism and design shows. They are decidedly different from the herd in their internationalism and wry take on a world visited rather than read about.
monocle.com/radio

❶
Kiosks
Finest purveyors of print

Where to "read all about it", then? **❶** *Rococo* in Notting Hill has been done up recently but hasn't lost its Aladdin's Cave aesthetic. If you're looking for an authentic outdoor kiosk (albeit an overgrown one) go to **❷** *AT Terry* on Great Marlborough Street opposite Liberty – well stocked, staunchly international and run by a knowledgeable guvnor. **❸** *Charlotte Street News* is in the heart of adland and is therefore rammed with men with hangovers looking for ideas to steal (and who knows: maybe it's lucky for playing the lottery, too?). If in Paddington, be sure to stop by the very first **❹** *Kioskafé*, which is supported by MONOCLE, for a latte and a selection of magazines and newspapers.

WHERE TO FIND THEM

01   Rococo: 12 Elgin Crescent, W11 2HX
     +44 (0)20 7727 5209
02   AT Terry: Great Marlborough Street, W1F 7JD
     +44 (0)20 7287 3312
03   Charlotte Street News: 66 Charlotte Street, W1T 4QE
     +44 (0)20 7636 4270
04   Kioskafé: 31 Norfolk Place, W2 1QH

②
Print frontrunners
Capital's best mags

London doesn't know if it's a young, cool, well-designed guru of films, art and music or a musty, moody, Oxbridge-educated, riotously rude and funny news nut – and neither does its media. The two best magazines to sum up this push-me-pull-you dichotomy are the beautifully designed film magazine *Little White Lies*, that takes a different film or director for its monthly theme, and *Private Eye*, the funniest magazine in London (and therefore the world). Yet the latter prints its satire on toilet roll with a layout straight from a malfunctioning typewriter. You choose but be sure to buy them both.

Design and architecture
—— London at its most striking

London's reputation as one of the world's most important design capitals is well deserved. There are few other cities to have contributed quite so much to so many sectors: fashion, graphics, architecture, furniture, branding. But what makes London so special is its international flavour: it has long been a place that attracts young talent from around the world thanks to its world-class educational facilities and exciting communities of masterly designers.

Beyond that, its status as a design capital is visible everywhere, from the street signs to the Underground stations, to its incredibly diverse architecture and even its cemeteries. The city's status as the centre of the world for so many years – not to mention its tumultuous and layered history – has played itself out very interestingly on the streetscape and skyline. Here are some of our favourite spots.

①

30 Cannon Street, City of London
Heritage worthy

This distinctive triangular office building on Cannon Street in London's financial centre was designed by Whinney, Son & Austen Hall and completed in 1977. Commissioned by French bank Crédit Lyonnais, it occupies the site of a former Victorian fire station. The signature cladding units of the façade were cast from glass fibre-reinforced concrete. It was the first building in the world to use this technique on such a large scale. As of 2015, 30 Cannon Street is rightfully on England's National Heritage list.
30 Cannon Street, EC4M 6YQ

②

No 1 Poultry, City of London
Loud and proud

Postmodernism – the fruity architectural style popular in the late 1970s and 1980s – may get a bad rap but there's plenty of good examples alive and well in the City to admire. No 1 Poultry, next to Bank junction, is one of our favourites. It's a salmon-pink and brick-red limestone beast, designed by Sir James Stirling like a cathedral of commerce, mashing up all sorts of different architectural reference points in a unique – and often misunderstood – fashion. Local bankers like it for a rooftop lunch (at the Coq d'Argent); we like it for its sheer verve and sense of humour.
No 1 Poultry, EC2R 8EJ

I've discovered new-found admiration for Poultry

Chalcot Square,
Primrose Hill

London has many beautiful squares – and plenty of pastel-coloured streets – but Chalcot Square in Primrose Hill is where they both collide. It's lined with broad, brightly coloured houses in a rainbow of technicolour shades and has been used in numerous films aiming to show London at its most quaint. Although it is the epitome of charming, those looking for something beyond surface value might note the lilac edifice in which Sylvia Plath lived.
Chalcot Square, NW1 8YA

③
Time & Life building,
Mayfair
Artistic licence

Set on the corner of Bruton and New Bond streets in Mayfair, the Time & Life building was constructed between 1951 and 1953 to house the British headquarters of the US publisher. Designed by Michael Rosenauer with interiors by Sir Hugh Casson and Misha Black, the seven-storey art deco façade was placed on the National Heritage list in 1988. It sports four cast-in-stone abstract sculptures by Henry Moore integrated into the exterior of the building's terrace, while a nickel-bronze sculpture by Maurice Lambert is mounted above the entrance.

Even though the publisher moved on in 1993, the building kept its name and is now home to various businesses, including the Hermès megastore on the ground floor.
153-137 New Bond Street/1 Bruton Street, W1J 6TL.

The height of fashion
—

Most shoppers keep their eyes at ground level when walking down Bond Street. Take your eyes off the shops and look up – the façades above Mulberry and Salvatore Ferragamo are especially becoming.

Interwar buildings
Modern masterpieces

ROYAL INSTITUTE OF BRITISH ARCHITECTS

①
Riba building, Fitzrovia
Architecture's home turf

The home of the Royal Institute
of British Architects (Riba) on 66
Portland Place was completed in
1934 after a competition to mark
the organisation's 100th anniversary.
The winning entrant was George
Grey Wornum's modernist-meets-
classically inspired design. This
building is decorated with stylised
sculptures and frescoes and is a
much-loved landmark in this part
of town. The boxy and extravagant
exterior belies an interior that is
high in art deco charm. Exquisite
finishing with charismatic attention
to detail is a constant theme inside.

You'd be forgiven for thinking
the frosted and etched glass, the
bronze and the shapely black marble
pillars of the stairwell recall a bygone
seafaring age. Wornum actually
went on to design the interiors of
the Cunard White Star Line's
RMS Queen Elizabeth.
66 Portland Place, W1B 1AD
+44 (0)20 7307 3888
ribavenues.com

It's often
been said
that my
beard is
very art
deco

②
Hoover Building, Ealing
Clean lines

One of the capital's finest art
deco landmarks can be found
in the most unlikely of places.
A 40-minute drive from central
London, towering over Ealing's
A40, stands the 1932-built Hoover
Building, designed by architecture
firm Wallis, Gilbert and Partners.
At the time the 24,000 sq m space
built for the US-founded vacuum-
cleaner company was hailed as
a palace of industry.

The building's monumental
façade, adorned with large
turquoise windows and geometric
patterns, pays tribute to Victorian
industrial buildings while hailing
the mechanised, modern world that
gave rise to the Hoover (as vacuum
cleaners are still called in the UK).

A long way from its romantic
beginnings this factory, which
once employed 3,000 people,
ended up closing down in
the 1980s and has since been
reincarnated as a supermarket.
Western Avenue, UB6 8DW

③
Highpoint Building, Highgate
Cubist cool

Highpoint One, the first and largest
building in this two-part complex,
was finished in 1935 by Russian
émigré and pioneer of international
modernism in Britain, Berthold
Lubetkin. The guiding principle
was Le Corbusier's Architectural
Promenade: the notion that the
architect created vistas and
compositions for the user to
walk into and through.

Every corner of Highpoint is
something of a modernist odyssey.
The sweeping canopy that acts as
an entrance to Highpoint Two is
supported by two caryatid figures,
facsimiles of those found at the
Acropolis. Lubetkin intended these
to soften the juxtaposition between
the nature outside and the building's
hard cubism. The residential
complex is not accessible to the
public apart from on the annual
open days in September (or you
could try your luck and ask the
porter politely).
North Hill, Highgate, N6 4BA

④
Lawn Road Flats, Hampstead
Modernism's white knight

Also known as the Isokon Flats,
this heritage-protected masterpiece
found on Lawn Road in verdant
Hampstead, commissioned by Jack
and Molly Pritchard, was designed
by architect Wells Coates in 1934.
Envisioned as an experiment in
urban living inspired by Le
Corbusier's concept of "machines
for living", the white concrete
monolith comprised 36 flats.
Designed for maximum utility in
the minimum floorspace, it housed
avant-garde royalty including
Bauhaus founder Walter Gropius
and novelist Agatha Christie.

Having fallen into disrepair
in the 1970s it has been restored
since as one of Britain's most
significant modernist structures
and is now home to the Isokon
Gallery, which gives visitors an
insight into its history and the
local modern movement.
*The Isokon Gallery, Lawn Road,
Hampstead, NW3 2XD
isokongallery.co.uk*

Bricked-up windows

When you're out stomping
around the squares and
avenues of London's grandest
neighbourhoods, you might
spot a number of bricked-up
windows in older buildings.
Why? In 1696, King William III
implemented a tax charging
families for every window in
their house. To avoid it, many
Londoners blocked up windows
that weren't totally necessary
to let light in, such as on
stairwells or in smaller rooms.
The charge, similar to
fenestration taxes in Scotland
and France, was lifted in 1851.

Ivory tower
—
The Isokon's
stairwell
encapsulates
the era

Penguin Pool, London Zoo

Berthold Lubetkin invested the
same level of care and material
considerations in his animal
clients at London Zoo as he did
the human apartment dwellers
at Highpoint (*see opposite
page*). The 1934 Penguin Pool
has an elliptical plan and spiral
interlocking ramps. As well as
being guided by functional
needs to create swimming,
feeding and resting areas,
Lubetkin wanted to create an
Antarctica in miniature.
*ZSL London Zoo,
Regent's Park, NW1 4RY
zsl.org*

5
2 Willow Road, Hampstead
Visionary living

In 1939, Hungarian-born architect Ernö Goldfinger moved into his new permanent home at 2 Willow Road. Goldfinger also designed the interior and most of the furniture himself and the property – bequeathed to the National Trust in 1995 – also contains much of the architect's art collection, including works by Duchamp, Henry Moore and Bridget Riley.

The style of the house, which is craftsy and residential but unashamedly modern, is said to have caused outrage among local residents, including the writer of the James Bond series Ian Fleming. It's therefore perhaps no coincidence that he went on to give his neighbour's name to one of his baddest of baddies.
2 Willow Road, Hampstead, NW3 1TH
+44 (0)20 7435 6166
nationaltrust.org.uk

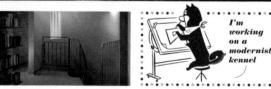

I'm working on a modernist kennel

Postwar buildings
Lasting impression

① Royal College of Physicians,
Regent's Park
Block party

Opened by Queen Elizabeth II
in 1964, the Royal College of
Physicians (RCP) was designed
by one of Britain's most important
modernist masters. Sir Denys
Lasdun went on to create late
modern and brutalist greats such
as the National Theatre and
countless academic megastructures
but this building is generally
considered his best.

Lasdun was asked by the college
if, with modern techniques, he
could provide "grace, elegance and
charm" that was in harmony with
John Nash's Georgian surrounds.
That he did, and the RCP is as
much a technical achievement as
an aesthetic one. At the front, a
cluster of three slender beams
supports the vast stretch of the
library. During construction, steel
was made extra tight to prevent
sagging in the decades to come.
Lasdun's creation is as taught,
crisp and beautiful as ever.
11 St Andrews Place, NW1 4LE
+44 (0)20 3075 1649
rcplondon.ac.uk

② Balfron Tower, Poplar,
and Trellick Tower,
North Kensington
Future fantastic

The issue of housing its growing
population in a well-designed
and affordable manner has long
been London's bête noire. This
was certainly the case in the
immediate postwar period and
it was architect Ernö Goldfinger
(*see opposite page*) who most
prominently took up the challenge.
The two towers he created – the
Balfron (1967) in London's east
and Trellick (1972) in the west –
still stand as almost symmetrical
monuments to a brave new era of
social housing.

Once Balfron was built,
Goldfinger and his wife Ursula
moved into flat NO 130 for two
months to try out this new
high-rise life for size. However,
the couple's socially conscious
intentions and their champagne
receptions with their council tenant
neighbours did not go down
well with the press of the time.

Both the towers are now
protected, although Trellick has
fared better in terms of keeping
its original social tenure.
Balfron Tower, St Leonard's Road,
E14 0QT;
Trellick Tower, 7 Golborne Road,
W10 5NY;

**Jean Cocteau mural in Notre
Dame De France Church,
Leicester Square**

In 1956, French poet, designer,
novelist and playwright Jean
Cocteau received an honorary
doctorate from University
of Oxford with the support
of then cultural attaché
René Varin. When Cocteau
asked what he could do in
return, Varin suggested he
decorate this church's
chapel. The resulting work
is totally enchanting.
Notre Dame De France
Church, 5 Leicester Place,
WC2H 7BX

3

Barbican, City of London
Design for life

The act of rebuilding London after
the Second World War saw many
great developments spring up, but
none quite so fine as the Barbican.
The complex – which includes
residences, schools, a museum
and an arts centre – took 20 years
to build across the 1960s and
1970s and was masterminded by
architects Chamberlin, Powell &
Bon, who also designed the Golden
Lane Estate next door (equally
worth a look around).

Barbican is one of the most
successful examples of brutalism;
perhaps no surprise bearing in
mind it took the architects seven
drafts to come up with the final
vision (at one point a glass pyramid
was mooted). Design-minded
visitors should also pay attention to
the Barbican's branding, courtesy of
London agency Studio North, and
book in for one of the regular tours
to properly discover what makes
this development so unique.
Silk Street, EC2Y 8DS

Pride of place
—
Barbican
houses more
than 4,000
residents

Stations
The Underground's visual highlights

① Arnos Grove, Piccadilly line
Surface value

Arnos Grove Underground station was opened in 1932 and although it was the work of Charles Holden – the foremost British architect of the interwar period – it was commissioned by someone who could reasonably be called London's greatest unsung hero: transport administrator Frank Pick. The Underground Board's then publicity officer had a passion for design and architecture. Pick and Holden toured Europe seeking inspiration and best practice before setting to work on the Piccadilly line extension, the last station of which was then Finsbury Park.

Holden's result is considered a masterpiece of modernist simplicity: a cylindrical ticket hall sits atop a square structure. The interior is equally noble, refined and, like most of Holden's works, pleasingly restrained. It is said that Pick would regularly inspect stations and would not be shy about ordering the removal of unwanted visual clutter. No doubt much in that regard would annoy Pick today – or possibly make his head explode – but Arnos Grove still represents 20th-century British architecture at its best.
Bowes Road, N11 1AN

② Cockfosters, Piccadilly line
Geometry lesson

If some of architect Charles Holden's Piccadilly line stations are all about what's visible at street level (*see previous entry*) then Cockfosters is a trackside revelation.

A cantilevered canopy spans the station's length, with its elegant structural support forming an intriguing concrete ribcage of a train shed. The point at which the long shed narrows to form a geometric arrowhead of sorts is the stuff of architectural fantasies. (The ease in which Holden seems to have devised such ingenious station designs is testament to his talents.) Cockfosters is also worth visiting for its original light and sign fittings and paintwork that, without being twee, takes passengers straight back to 1933, the year of completion. Particularly attractive are the hanging lamps and "way out" signs that employ the Johnston Sans font that was used for the station's opening.
Cockfosters Road, EN4 0DZ

③ Westminster, Jubilee line
Cavern club

It might be Big Ben and the Houses of Parliament that draw the majority of crowds to the area but what lies underneath is equally magnificent. Completed in 1999 as part of interconnected architecture and infrastructure projects, Westminster Station is a marvel of civic engineering.

Michael Hopkins & Partners designed both the station and the new parliamentary offices of Portcullis House that are directly above. Supporting columns to this structure pierce the 30-metre-tall cavern that was carved out to accommodate the Jubilee line below.

A complex structure of beams and buttresses dominate the inspiring if slightly menacing space. All that Underground passengers need to do is look up, down or over the side as escalators thread gracefully through the structure.
Bridge Street, SW1A 2JR

Bridges
Scenic ways to cross the river

① Waterloo Bridge
Stone-clad simplicity

The structure that straddles the Thames between Blackfriars Bridge and Hungerford Bridge was designed by Sir Giles Gilbert Scott (grandson of Victorian architect Sir George Gilbert Scott).

It was built to replace an older structure that had been deemed unsafe and was constructed using reinforced concrete and granite cut from the original bridge.

Simple in outline and without ornamentation, Waterloo Bridge is in keeping with its surroundings and affords fantastic views up and down the river. It's also the best approach to the South Bank's concrete treasures such as the National Theatre.
Nearest Underground: Waterloo or Embankment

② Albert Bridge
Jewel of the Thames

The Albert Bridge connects Chelsea with Battersea in the south and is a unique hybrid of a suspension bridge and cantilevered bridge. Two dramatic turreted arches support what poet John Betjeman described as "one of the beauties of the London river". It's as pretty as you'd expect for this part of town.
Nearest Underground: Sloane Square

③ Blackfriars Railway Bridge
Solar sensation

London-based Pascall+Watson has transformed Blackfriars on the north of the Thames into a river-spanning station bridge. Its 4,400 photovoltaic panels provide up to half of the station's energy and make this reinterpretation of the traditional river crossing the world's largest solar-powered bridge.
Nearest Underground: Blackfriars or Southwark

Cemeteries
London's historic graveyards

Back from the dead

In the late 18th and 19th centuries, gothic revivalism was one of the defining movements in western architecture. In England it was particularly pronounced and has become known as the Victorian gothic movement (named after Queen Victoria, who lent her name to so much during this period). The recently renovated St Pancras railway station is a perfect example of the style. But this intellectual and aesthetic revolution also coincided with a demographic one: a boom in the population of the nation's cities, a spike in the number of deaths and a subsequent urgent need for more cemeteries.

As a result, London has a number of enormous cemeteries dating back to the era, many with neo-gothic features, dotted around what was once the periphery of the city. They provide a fascinating insight into London's past and, from an architectural standpoint, remain as startlingly well-preserved examples of the gothic revival.

① Nunhead
Gothic genius

Nunhead Cemetery, situated south of the river in the borough of Southwark, was opened in 1840 and remains one of London's little-known gems. The stunning gothic Anglican chapel, built in 1844, is a must-see, as are the uninterrupted views across London to St Paul's Cathedral, which can be glimpsed through breaks in the trees.
Linden Grove, SE15 3LP
fonc.org.uk

② Brompton
Till death do us art

Brompton Cemetery is one of the so-called Magnificent Seven: a collection of some of the oldest cemeteries in London. The site in west London (near Earls Court) houses some 35,000 monuments, from simple headstones to huge mausoleums, 28 of which are on the National Heritage list for England.

Highlights include the domed chapel, the Leyland tomb by Victorian artist Edward Burne-Jones and the headstone of suffragette Emmeline Pankhurst.
Fulham Road, SW10 9UG
royalparks.org.uk

I hope my final nesting place is as grand as this

Highgate
Meeting of minds

Divided in two, Highgate Cemetery's west side is the older half, dating back to 1839. Here among the ivy-encrusted tombs and vaults you'll find Egyptian Avenue where notable Victorian families are buried, the ornate mausoleum of Julius Beer and the gothic-style Terrace Catacombs. It's a breathtaking theme park of morbidity and legend has it the Victorians would hold tea parties among the dead (nowadays you need to join one of the regular tours to gain access). On the other side is the east cemetery where Karl Marx, Lucian Freud and George Eliot are all interred.
Swain's Lane, N6 6PJ
highgatecemetery.org

Dead popular
———
Highgate has approximately 55,000 graves

Thames Barrier, Woolwich

The Thames Barrier was built in 1982 to protect central London from the risk of flooding caused by tidal surges. It was constructed by Rendel, Palmer and Tritton and is the world's second-largest movable flood barrier after Oosterscheldekering in the Netherlands. The striking stainless-steel cladding on the 10 gates is best viewed when reflecting the glow of sunset.
1 Unity Way, Woolwich SE18 5NJ

Tate & Lyle sugar refinery, Silvertown

Silvertown's position near the mouth of the Thames means its history is defined by industry. There had been many sugar refiners operating here but when Henry Tate and Abram Lyle merged in 1921 they created one of the British Empire's most iconic brands. Rising above the terraces, the Tate & Lyle sugar refinery is one of the largest in the world. Be sure to spot it on the landing into nearby City Airport.
Factory Road, Silvertown, E16 2EW

Design museums and galleries
London's must-see collections

① Geffrye Museum, Shoreditch
Home from home

Visitors looking for a glimpse of Londoners' homes through the ages should take a trip down to the Geffrye Museum in Shoreditch. "Our displays of London living rooms and gardens from 1600 reflect changes in society, patterns of behaviour, style and taste," says curator Hannah Fleming.

It is laid out in chronological order and visitors start by stepping into restored parlours, which become drawing rooms, which turn into living rooms, before arriving at modern apartments. Attention has been paid to every detail to preserve an authentic feel. "Our aim is to spark imaginations and inspire people," says Fleming.
136 Kingsland Road, E2 8EA
+44 (0)20 7739 9893
geffrye-museum.org.uk

②
Sir John Soane's Museum, Holborn
Scholarly collection

Sir John Soane's Museum in Lincoln's Inn Fields (London's largest public square) occupies the former home and office of the renowned neoclassical architect, which was preserved as a museum by an act of parliament in 1833.

Stepping inside is like entering the kaleidoscopic world of the 19th-century visionary. Skylights illuminate his collection of architectural models, drawings and artefacts from his tour around the world, from the sarcophagus of King Seti I to paintings by Turner and Canaletto; there are also nearly 7,000 books, among them Shakespeare's First Folio.

"This is such an important place; Soane influences architects until today," says director Abraham Thomas, who recently restored the museum to former glory after a five-year refurbishment project.
13 Lincoln's Inn Fields, WC2A 3BP
+ 44 (0)20 7405 2107
soane.org

Oh, so you're a vegetarian Beefeater?

③
Design Museum, Bermondsey
Blueprint of the ages

Since 1989, London's Design Museum has been housed in a former banana warehouse just footsteps from Tower Bridge. "Knowing about design is important because it helps us think about what we might be able to achieve in the future," says senior curator Alex Newson of the museum's all-encompassing collection of the best in design, from fashion to technology.

Besides checking out the temporary exhibitions inside, don't miss the Tank enclosure used for installations on the waterfront.

The current building was modified in the Bauhaus tradition by local design firm Conran but after nearly three decades the Design Museum is looking to triple in size in late 2016 by moving to the former Commonwealth Institute building in Kensington.
28 Shad Thames, SE1 2YD
+ 44 (0)20 7403 6933
designmuseum.org

④
Museum of Brands, Packaging & Advertising, Notting Hill
That's a wrap

While most of us don't think twice before tossing out a sweet wrapper, British historian Robert Opie has been saving packaging for decades. He set up the Museum of Brands, Packaging and Advertising in 1984 to keep a record of how brand presentation has changed with consumer culture. "It's surprising that a subject so fundamental to our daily lives has not been fully understood," he says.

In 2005 the museum moved to a site in Notting Hill, where visitors today can browse more than 12,000 crisp packets, cereal boxes, drink cans and other examples of "throwaway history" dating back to the Victorian era. "Here is evidence of a consumer revolution that has transformed the way we live," says Opie.
2 Colville Mews, W11 2AR
+ 44 (0)20 7908 0880
museumofbrands.com

⑤
Galerie Kreo, Mayfair
Exciting lighting

On a grey and gloomy day head to Clémence and Didier Krzentowski's Galerie Kreo in Mayfair. The expansive lamp display at its 2014-opened London branch is guaranteed to brighten your day. "We are collectors of vintage lights and possess more than 800 pieces," says Didier Krzentowski, who co-founded Galerie Kreo in Paris in 1999.

Apart from showcasing lamps by the likes of Gino Sarfatti and Jacques Biny, the gallery displays limited-edition furniture creations by contemporary designers such as François Bauchet, Marc Newson, Jaime Hayon and Jasper Morrison, and acts as a design-research laboratory. "The pieces we produce and present are exclusive to our gallery," says Krzentowski. "Today we are the reference for 20th-century lighting."
14A Hay Hill, W1J 8NZ
+ 44 (0)20 7629 5954
galeriekreo.fr

⑥
The Building Centre, Fitzrovia
Dissecting construction

"We are trying to really fulfil our objective of making the world a better place through innovative design ideas," says Lewis Blackwell, the executive director of London's Building Centre. At its heart is the Pipers central London model, a 1:1,500 scale replica of central London measuring some 12 metres in length that – through highlighting proposed new developments – shows visitors what the city of the future will look like.

Although this alone makes The Building Centre worth a visit, there is plenty more on offer, too. The 1931-established charity is a space designed to inspire and inform architects, engineers, students and the public through exhibitions, talks and seminars showcasing and debating urban environment issues and projects. In urban planning and construction "you really need to think about the long-term and create design solutions by working with the community," says Blackwell. That's precisely the sentiment The Building Centre is hoping to foster.
26 Store Street, WC1E 7BT
+44 (0)20 7692 4000
buildingcentre.co.uk

New London Architecture

Located in the Building Centre in Fitzrovia (*see above*), New London Architecture is a free-entry forum for anyone keen on the built environment. There is a year-round programme of events so look out for great speakers, conferences and round-table discussions. The organisation, which produces the *New London Quarterly* magazine, also puts on exhibitions throughout the year on a range of topics from *Spans: Viaducts, Bridges & Walkways* to *Sustainable Cities*.

Specialist shops
Niche retail in the city

①
Stanley Gibbons, Covent Garden
Trading post

Dating back to 1856, Stanley Gibbons is the world's oldest rare-stamp merchant. Just opposite the Savoy on the Strand, it stocks more than one million stamps; the shop has the broadest collection in the world. In addition there is a selection of rare coins, tokens and bank notes available to browse and purchase. Stanley Gibbons also hosts up to 10 philatelic auctions per year.
399 Strand, WC2R 0LX
+44 (0)20 7836 8444
stanleygibbonsplc.com

②
Shepherds, Pimlico
Prints charming

This charming shop opened in 1973 and is all about printmaking, bookbinding and fine papers. The shelves are stocked with offerings from around the world including *Katazome-shi* (stencil-dyed paper using kimono-printing techniques), greeting cards and even small furnishings. More studious visitors can try a course in silkscreen printing or glueless binding.
30 Gillingham Street, SW1V 1HU
+44 (0)20 7233 9999
store.bookbinding.co.uk

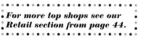

For more top shops see our Retail section from page 44.

Smithfield Market

Where the City of London and Farringdon meet has been the site for the Smithfield meat market for centuries. Although the east section is well kept and in use, the westernmost block – once the general market – is currently derelict. These ornate covered halls and curved buildings topped with *oeil-de-boeuf* windows make for a menagerie of urban topography in an otherwise sterile part of town. Developers are at constant war over the site's future so have a look while you can.
Snow Hill, EC1A 2AL

Signage
Getting around in style

①
London Underground map
Reading between the lines

Even the most seasoned London Underground navigator has to look at the Tube map every now and then. All 270 stations are clearly marked on 13 brightly coloured lines; it's an indispensible tool for plotting the fastest route across the capital and is practically foolproof. It might come as a surprise that the map's seemingly modern design traces its roots all the way back to 1933. Before this the Tube was mapped geographically, which proved cumbersome as more stations and lines were added to the network. So an engineering draughtsman for the London Underground called Harry Beck proposed to "tidy it up by straightening the lines, experimenting with diagonals and evening out the distance between stations".

It took some time for his bosses to pick up on the then radical solution, but when they eventually did, it stuck. Until this day Beck is credited on the map's bottom-right corner: "This diagram is an evolution of the original design conceived in 1931 by Harry Beck". Just don't be tempted to follow it as a pedestrian above ground: you will definitely get lost.

②
Jock Kinneir and Margaret Calvert
Sign of the times

At the turn of the 1960s, Britain's road signage, from motorways to tiny B-roads, was totally haphazard: there was no overarching body ensuring uniformity and no consistent design language. In a brave move the government of the day entrusted the job of coming up with a coherent and uniform system to Jock Kinneir, a well-established graphic designer, and his South Africa-born assistant Margaret Calvert.

The pair embarked on one of the most ambitious information design schemes in Britain's history and came up with a truly exemplary road signage system that is still – rightly – lauded and emulated around the world. Featuring a brand new typeface and maps oriented towards the driver, the new signs were rolled out across the country from 1958 and can still be seen directing drivers on London's streets.

③
Legible London
Not-so-pedestrian design

The British capital is a great city for getting lost in but sometimes you don't have that luxury if you are pressed for time. To serve those who would rather walk than travel by Tube, Transport for London commissioned Legible London in 2004. The award-winning pedestrian way-finding system was designed by Applied Information Group in close collaboration with Lacock Gullam and manufactured by Woodhouse.

You'll see these signs all around the city (there are roughly 1,300 in total to date): upright maps made from stainless steel with vitreous enamel panels illustrating the local area and estimating walking times to nearby landmarks. Before Legible London there were no fewer than 32 separate pedestrian sign systems in central London – the new technique has decluttered the streets and created a coherent, consistent and very welcome signage system.

Sport and fitness

—— Health kicks

London has the infrastructure in place to be a great city for healthy living. It is one of the greenest cities in the world with several centrally located parks crisscrossed by pedestrianised tree-lined paths; it has meandering canals that offer those looking to escape the hustle and bustle a peaceful, tranquil haven. There are even natural ponds to swim in (as long as you're willing to brave the icy water).

Across these pages we set out the best ways to make the most of this bounty and stay in shape during your visit to the British capital. Although you might just want to hit the hotel gym and the sauna, we recommend making the most of the great outdoors (anyone for tennis?) while exploring the city at the same time. And if getting a trim is as important to you as keeping trim, consult our list of barbers and hairdressers on page 125.

Swimming pools
Make a splash

①
Marshall Street Leisure Centre, Soho
Art deco diving

Most of the swimming pools in central London are locked away in gyms that ask for lengthy and expensive memberships. But the Marshall Street Leisure Centre, an art deco gem, is open to the public on a pay-as-you-go basis. There has been a public bath here since 1850 and this building was reopened in 2010 after an £11m renovation. The marble features and barrel-vaulted ceiling have been retained but new changing rooms have been added for the 30-metre pool.
15 Marshall Street, W1F 7EL.
+44 (0)20 7871 7222
better.org.uk/leisure/marshall-street-leisure-centre

②
The Berkeley Hotel, Knightsbridge
Luxury lengths

If you're looking for a relaxing place to have a dip rather than a serious work-out, try the rooftop pool at the Berkeley Hotel in Knightsbridge. This is one of the best-kept secrets in the capital: a pool in a perfect location with views over Hyde Park. While it's reserved for hotel guests at the weekend, the pool is open to the public on weekdays from 06.00 to 22.00. Handily, the day pass also includes access to the spa and wellness centre.
Wilton Place, SW1X 7RL
+44 (0)20 7235 6000
the-berkeley.co.uk

Outdoor swimming

The weather in London seldom warrants a dip in an outdoor unheated pool but the English are famous for their imperviousness to frosty temperatures. So if you want to do as some locals do, here are three of the best outdoor pools in the capital.

01 Serpentine: Top of the list has to be the Serpentine, the lake in the centre of Hyde Park. The swimming area and paddling pool are open seven days a week throughout the summer months (June to mid-September) and every weekend in May. This is also home to the Serpentine Swimming Club, the oldest in the UK.
royalparks.org.uk

02 Hampstead Heath: There are three swimming ponds on Hampstead Heath: one for women, one for men and one mixed. They are open to the public every day of the year and supervised by a lifeguard.
cityoflondon.gov.uk

03 Parliament Hill: The heritage-protected outdoor lido at Parliament Hill (at the southern end of Hampstead Heath) is a great spot for an outdoor swim but it gets busy with children during the summer months, so head over early to get a few lengths in. The hot showers will make up for the brisk waters.
cityoflondon.gov.uk

_I hope
the ice
has
thawed..._

Hotel gyms
Fit for travel

①

The Langham, Marylebone
Grand hotel health club

The five-star Langham hotel has been a landmark of the West End since 1865 and its modern health-and-fitness facilities are just as luxurious as its historic halls. Hotel guests escaping the bustle of neighbouring Oxford Street can enjoy the tranquility of Langham's Health Club and Spa, while those visiting can buy a two-week membership for £150.

The gym is equipped with TechnoGym cross-trainers, rowing machines, treadmills and cycles and there are personal trainers on hand. After a workout, unwind in the Chuan Spa with its 16-metre heated indoor pool. The Chinese-inspired wellness area is also fitted with a salt sauna and steam rooms. Treatments available at the spa range from the 90-minute Traveller's Retreat to the three-hour Serenity Shen massage-and-facial package.
*1C Portland Place, Regent Street,
W1B 1JA
+44 (0)20 7636 1000
london.langhamhotels.co.uk*

Three more

01 Shoreditch House and Hotel: Hotel guests enjoy the spacious Fourth Floor Gym in east London's members' club with its steam room, sauna and TechnoGym machines. There's also a 16-metre rooftop pool ideal for lazy summer days as well as pilates, yoga, circuits and Nike training club classes.
shoreditchhouse.com

02 Four Seasons at Park Lane, Mayfair: Ascend to the 10th floor and you'll find yourself at this rooftop sanctuary with a spa and fitness centre with views of the Houses of Parliament.
fourseasons.com/london

03 The Library Gym, Notting Hill: For longer stays try this Notting Hill gym: an old synagogue transformed into a boutique gym for literary types (books adorn the walls). Try the 15-minute classes for the quickest fix of endorphins.
thelibrarygym.com

Cycling
Life on two wheels

①

Regent's Canal, north London
Waterside cycling route

A great way to discover the city is by cycling along the peaceful banks of Regent's Canal. Completed in 1820, the 14km-long canal harks back to a time when these waterways were the city's arteries. Fuel up at one of the many food joints in ❶*Little Venice*, just north of Paddington, and follow the canal through Regent's Park, past ❷*London Zoo* and the stalls of ❸*Camden Lock Market*. Roughly an hour later, finish up at ❹*Broadway Market* in east London; on Saturdays it is the site of a bustling food market.

STARTING POINT: Blomfield Road, Little Venice, W2 1TH
NOTE: Cycling maps are available at *tfl.gov.uk*

Ticket to ride

Bloomsbury's Cloud 9 Cycles is an independent bike shop moments from the British Museum. The staff build bespoke bikes but also rent them out to visitors, each with lights, lock, helmet and puncture-proof tyres.
cloud9cycles.com

The great outdoors

Depending on the season there is a whole host of other ways to get a breath of fresh air and stay healthy in the capital without hitting the gym.

01 Ice skating: Around Christmas, London gets its skates on as ice rinks pop up across the capital. Our top pick is the rink at Somerset House – but there are great pop-ups outside the Natural History Museum and at Broadgate, too. *somersethouse.org.uk*

02 Rowing: From April through to September it's possible to hire rowing boats and pedalos on the Serpentine in Hyde Park. *royalparks.org.uk*

03 Horse riding: The Hyde Park Stables are open all year round and offer members of the public the chance to hire horses and ponies for rides through London's historic park. *hydeparkstables.com*

All-rounder
Buzzing sports hub

①

Olympic Park, Stratford
Lasting legacy

Part of London's bid to secure the 2012 Olympics was a promise to open the venues' doors to members of the public after the event. The site now welcomes visitors year-round and there are dozens of state-of-the-art sports arenas to explore. Take a dip in the 50-metre pool at Zaha Hadid's London Aquatics Centre; swing a racket at the Lee Valley Hockey and Tennis Centre, which encompasses four indoor and six outdoor tennis courts; or race around the 6,000-seat velodrome where Sir Chris Hoy became the most successful British Olympian of all time. Two-wheelers are available for rent for those interested in taking a turn or riding the 8km mountain bike trail.

There is also the Arcelor Mittal Orbit sculpture by Sir Anish Kapoor. Although the art world is still divided on its aesthetic merits, at 115 metres it is the tallest piece of public art in Britain and offers panoramic views of the city.

Food and drink is available at stalls across the park and at the Timber Lodge Café. This relatively new east London destination is worth a visit and the best way to get here is via the Underground towards Stratford Station.
Queen Elizabeth Olympic Park, E20 2ST
+44 (0)800 072 2110
queenelizabetholympicpark.co.uk

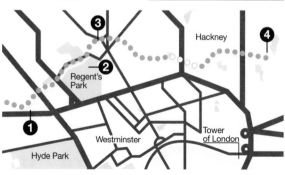

Tennis
Rally up

①

Will to Win, Camden/Westway Sports & Fitness, Kensington
Top service

In the height of summer there is nowhere better to play a game of tennis than in the beautiful surrounds of Regent's Park. The 12 hard courts are complemented by changing rooms, a café and a sports shop. If it's pouring with rain, despair not: head to Westway Sports & Fitness in west London, where there are eight indoor acrylic courts and you can pay as you play.
York Bridge, Regent's Park, NW1 4NU
+ 44 (0)20 7486 4216
willtowin.co.uk
1 Crowthorne Road, W10 6RP
+ 44 (0)20 8969 0992
sports.westway.org

I think I'll stick to a simple game of fetch

Net gain
——
Will to Win has courts in many royal parks

Hair care and grooming

01 Ted's Grooming Room, Fitzrovia: There are nine of these Ted Baker outposts in London, including two in upmarket Fitzrovia. The latest addition to the set is this one on Mortimer Street, which opened in January 2015. We also love the Ottoman Lounge in Holborn for a clean Turkish shave.
tedsgroomingroom.com

02 Pankhurst London, Mayfair: This barbershop on Newburgh Street, behind Carnaby Street, is watched over by successful men's stylist Brent Pankhurst. The grooming products are all own-brand and infused with his signature bay rum and lime scent.
pankhurstlondon.com

03 Joe and Co, Soho: Sharp haircuts and all-round barber service off Berwick Street in the heart of Soho. The atmosphere is unfussy and informal thanks to the colourful fit-out by London-based design studio Hyperkit.
joeandco.net

04 Graffiti, Mayfair: Japanese-inspired unisex salon in Mayfair. Get the deep conditioning treatment for suitably moisturised and nourished hair; for an immaculate Japanese cut make a booking with Shunji Watanabe.
graffiti.ashair.co.uk

05 Rossano Ferretti, Mayfair: Housed in the vaults of a 1740s mansion next to the Ritz hotel, this salon offers top-notch ladies' cuts and haircare while a chef prepares Italian dishes on site.
rossanoferretti.com

Running routes
Upping the pace

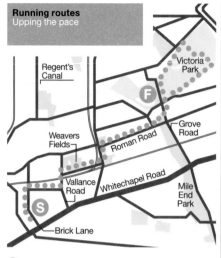

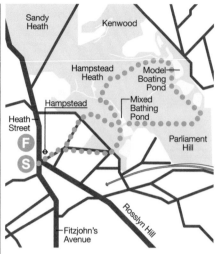

①

Victoria Park, Hackney and Tower Hamlets
Circle the people's park

DISTANCE: 6.7km
GRADIENT: Flat
DIFFICULTY: Hard
HIGHLIGHT: Running through Victoria Park with its
  picturesque pond
BEST TIME: Sunday morning, pre-market
NEAREST UNDERGROUND: Aldgate East, Aldgate

The first of our recommended running routes takes
you through a pleasant pocket of one of London's most
rapidly changing districts: Hackney. Start on Brick
Lane, traditionally the heart of the capital's Bangladeshi
community, where on Sunday mornings you'll find
market sellers setting up their stalls. Head north, turn
right on Buxton Street and zigzag via Vallance Road,
Dunbridge Street and Three Colts Lane. Run through
Bethnal Green Gardens and come out onto Roman
Road. This will take you over the beginning of Regent's
Canal and across Wennington Green.

Next turn left onto Grove Road and follow it
to the entrance of Victoria Park, one of the prettiest
parks in inner London and the epicentre of a wave of
gentrification. Enter the park and turn right, keeping
the Hertford Union Canal on your right-hand side.
Complete the best part of a full circuit of the park
before cutting down to the Pavilion Café. Stop here
and reward yourself with a hearty breakfast.

: **Where to buy**
:
: Our top picks for running gear in the capital:
: NikeLab (*nike.com/nikelab*) in Shoreditch, east
: London, and Runners Need (*runnersneed.com*).

②

Hampstead Heath, Hampstead
Head into the wild

DISTANCE: 4.8km
GRADIENT: Steep inclines in parts
DIFFICULTY: Hard
HIGHLIGHT: The wildness of Hampstead Heath stands
  in contrast to the manicured parks of central
  London
BEST TIME: Any time on a weekday to experience the
  park at its quietest
NEAREST UNDERGROUND: Hampstead

This run starts and ends in Hampstead, which to
the uninitiated might seem a schlep from the heart
of the city but it's only a few Underground stops to
get here. Hampstead is one of the most pleasant and
salubrious neighbourhoods in London and is right
on the doorstep of Hampstead Heath, a vast, wild
expanse of green space that feels a million miles
from the hustle and bustle of the city.

Start at Hampstead Underground and head straight
down Flask Walk before turning onto Willow Road and
ducking to your left onto the heath. Run across East
Heath Road and take the next right, a path that will take
you uphill to the junction with Lime Avenue.

From here, run round the circumference of the
heath, taking right turns when you reach the outer
perimeters. On the eastern edge of the park, keep the
three large ponds on your left-hand side. In this corner
you'll spot the Stone of Free Speech on your left, a squat
white obelisk that was the focal point of political and
religious meetings in the early 19th century. When you
get to the southwestern corner of the heath, take the path
that bisects another two ponds and cross back over East
Heath Road as you exit. Run down Well Walk, which
will take you back to the centre of Hampstead; reward
yourself with breakfast at Ginger and White.

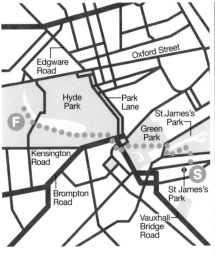

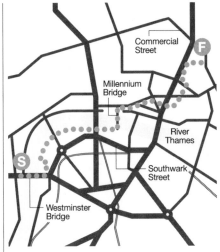

③
Central London Parks, City of Westminster
Regal wave and a run

DISTANCE: 4km
GRADIENT: Flat
DIFFICULTY: Easy
HIGHLIGHT: Going past Buckingham Palace and the Victoria Memorial
BEST TIME: Early morning at the weekend to avoid the flocks of tourists
NEAREST UNDERGROUND: St James's Park, Victoria

This route takes in some of the most iconic monuments in central London, as well as three of the most scenic parks: St James's, Green Park and, of course, Hyde Park.

Start at St James's Park Underground station and head straight down Queen Anne's Gate into St James's Park itself. Take the path straight ahead of you until you hit the small, picturesque lake in the centre; at this point turn left rather than crossing the bridge and then run a quarter-circuit before exiting in the northwestern corner.

Cross The Mall and be sure to cast your gaze westward to Buckingham Palace and the Victoria Memorial. Then make your way onto Constitution Hill, keeping Green Park on your right until you reach the roundabout at Hyde Park Corner and the Wellington Arch, built between 1825 and 1827. This is one of London's busiest intersections so your best bet is to follow the underpass and enter Hyde Park in the southeastern corner.

Follow signs for the Serpentine, the beautiful lake in the heart of the park where numerous events took place during the London 2012 Olympics. Do half a lap of the lake heading clockwise and finish up at the Serpentine Gallery (*see page 99*) on the lake's western edge for a well-earned rest.

④
The Southbank, Southwark
Architectural tour

DISTANCE: 5.6km
GRADIENT: Flat
DIFFICULTY: Medium
HIGHLIGHT: Running across Millennium Bridge with St Paul's Cathedral straight ahead
BEST TIME: Mid-morning; avoid rush hour
NEAREST UNDERGROUND: Westminster, St James's Park

This is a running route for architecture aficionados. Start by the clock tower that houses Big Ben at the Houses of Parliament (designed by Sir Charles Barry) and head south straight across the Thames over Westminster Bridge.

Once you hit the southern bank, turn left at the stone statue of a lion – known as the Coade stone – and run along Southbank past the London Aquarium and iconic riverside landmarks such as the Royal Festival Hall, the brutalist National Theatre and the Oxo Tower. When you reach the Tate Modern with its brick façade and single towering chimney, cross back over the river onto the north bank via the Millennium Bridge. As you bounce across you will be afforded a spectacular view of St Paul's Cathedral.

Now you take a winding course through the City of London, the heart of the capital's financial district. First turn right, heading east, on Queen Victoria Street until you get to Bank Station and then duck down Lombard Street before taking a left onto Lime Street. This will take you past some of the most spectacular buildings in the City, including Lord Rogers' Lloyd's Building and the wonderfully nicknamed trio of the Gherkin, Cheese Grater and Walkie-Talkie towers. You'll now be within striking distance of Old Spitalfields Market, which is home to numerous places for coffee and a reviving breakfast.

Walks
—— Find your own London

London is a loose association of villages, a cluster of interwoven neighbourhoods that have their own distinct characters. The city has altered dramatically in recent years, with areas previously regarded a little warily emerging as artisan and culinary spots. Here are five urban walks that are perfect showcases of London's fresh developments alongside some grand traditions.

NEIGHBOURHOOD 01

Bermondsey
Riverside revival

Just south of the Thames, nestled between Southwark, Rotherhithe and Peckham, is Bermondsey. It has been quietly transformed in recent decades. It was once an integral point along London's waterways and a hub for the processing and trading of leather and hides; today the area's industrial past is still in evidence across a series of warehouse buildings that line the cobbled streets. Until the 1980s – when cash was pumped in as part of the London Docklands redevelopment – many of these buildings stood empty and derelict. The days of low rents for large spaces – which made Bermondsey a popular destination for artists pushed out of other parts of the city – may have passed but the area's creative history is still evident. Bristling with culture and good transport links to the City of London, the area is home to a number of galleries celebrating both established and emerging artists, as well as restaurants and bars that locals have tried – and failed – to keep secret.

The area is also known for its bustling markets. The antiques market on Bermondsey Square is a spectacle, bursting into life at dawn each Friday. It echoes the colourful cockney days of old and you'll find everything from furniture to cutlery and china. Borough Market to the west is a great spot to stock up on English produce at its best.

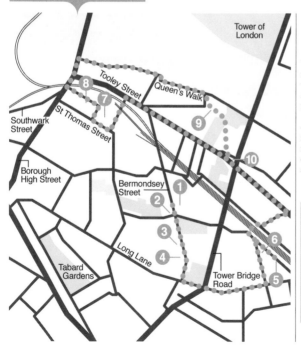

Culinary tour
Bermondsey walk

Starting at Bermondsey Underground, walk past the neat rows of former factories, a throwback to the area's former life as an industrial centre, and you'll find yourself on Bermondsey Street. This is a little-known culinary hub attracting both local residents and Londoners from further afield. If you arrive in the early morning, head for breakfast at ❶ *The Garrison*, one of London's

Getting there
——
Bermondsey Street is roughly equidistant between London Bridge and Bermondsey stations. Both are on the Jubilee line and the former is also on the Northern line. The 521 and 48 buses also go past London Bridge from Holborn and Hackney, respectively.

original and finest gastropubs. The award-winning, green-tiled venue serves a hearty English breakfast but there's also a berry smoothie and house muesli for the more health-conscious.

If it's Spanish fare you fancy, walk a couple of doors down to ❷ *José Tapas and Sherry Bar*. Open every day from 12.00, this cosy location serves faultless *pinchos*, such as platters of *gordal* olives and *chorizo al vino*. Staying on Bermondsey Street, next take in some contemporary culture at Jay Jopling's ❸ *White Cube*. The minimalist 1970s building by Casper Mueller Kneer Architects is one of the largest commercial-art spaces in the UK. Expect conceptual paintings, photography and sculpture from artists such as Gilbert & George and Damien

Hirst. For lunch pop into the super-sleek ❹ *Zucca*, a modern Italian restaurant run by River Café alumnus Sam Harris.

Bermondsey bursts into life at the weekend. On Saturday mornings many Londoners

migrate to ❺ *Maltby Street Market: Ropewalk*, located a short walk away under the old railway arches. Even if you're not hungry it's an ideal place to soak up some atmosphere. Rifle through the extensive antique offerings at the Lassco store or pop into the outpost of acclaimed British chef Fergus Henderson's ❻ *St John Bakery Room* to sample its always-popular custard doughnuts.

For panoramic views of the capital, head towards London Bridge Station and go up The Shard, London's 87-storey, Renzo Piano-designed structure. The tallest skyscraper in western Europe includes a selection of restaurants, bars and the Shangri-La Hotel. Rather than pay a king's ransom to go up in the lift to see the city from the building's viewing platform, pre-book a table at ❼ *Aqua Shard* for a cocktail on the 31st floor. On sunny days, head across to one of London's few lofty venues: ❽ *The Rooftop Café* at The Exchange. Don't let its stripped-back, office-block entrance put you off; this third-floor restaurant and terrace bar is a well-kept London secret.

To walk off a full stomach, stroll along the River Thames before popping your head around the door at ❾ *The Scoop Amphitheatre* on Queen's Walk, where everything from Christmas markets to film screenings are staged throughout the course of the year.

Finally, round off the day with dinner at ❿ *Restaurant Story*, one of London's finest food venues. It serves Michelin-starred cooking from chef Tom Sellers.

Address book

01 The Garrison
99-101 Bermondsey Street, SE1 3XB
+44 (0)20 7089 9355
thegarrison.co.uk

02 José Tapas and Sherry Bar
104 Bermondsey Street, SE1 3UB
+44 (0)20 7403 4902
josepizarro.com

03 White Cube
144-152 Bermondsey Street, SE1 3TQ
+44 (0)20 7930 5373
whitecube.com

04 Zucca
184 Bermondsey Street, SE1 3TQ
+44 (0)20 7378 6809
zuccalondon.com

05 Maltby Street Market: Ropewalk
Ropewalk, SE1 2HQ
maltby.st

06 St John Bakery Room
Arch 42, Ropewalk, SE1 2HQ
stjohngroup.uk.com

07 Aqua Shard
Level 31, The Shard, 31 St Thomas Street, SE1 9RY
+44 (0)20 3011 1256
aquashard.co.uk

08 The Rooftop Café
The Exchange, 28 London Bridge Street, SE1 9SG
+44 (0)20 3102 3770
therooftopcafe.co.uk

09 The Scoop Amphitheatre
Queen's Walk, SE1 2DB
+44 (0)20 7403 4866
morelondon.com

10 Restaurant Story
199 Tooley Street, SE1 2JX
+44 (0)20 7183 2117
restaurantstory.co.uk

NEIGHBOURHOOD 02
Hackney
Spit and polish

The speed with which the London Fields area of east London has been transformed from a site of urban decay to one of inner-city splendour is astonishing, yet the alteration itself is hardly surprising. London Fields is a small park that has become a local institution for lazy summer days thanks to its perfectly preserved lido and a wealth of bars and shops along nearby Broadway Market. Nestled to the northeast, the wide, leafy streets that crisscross this well-gentrified pocket of the city are home to some of the most beautiful examples of Victorian architecture.

Right in the heart of this district is Wilton Way. One of the most fashionable stretches in London, it is emblematic of the changes that have taken place across Hackney, a borough that was once synonymous with poverty, gun crime and disaffected youth. The cheap rents that the area used to offer encouraged creative entrepreneurs to set up shop here and no enclave of Hackney is more indicative of its fiercely independent spirit.

Over the course of a few years, this neighbourhood has been buffed and polished almost beyond recognition, to the amazement (and occasional dismay) of longstanding locals who have watched on in disbelief as newsagents and greasy-spoon cafés have been replaced by boutiques, artisan coffee shops and pop-up restaurants.

Diamonds in the rough
Hackney walk

Populated by artfully dishevelled hipsters, the borough of Hackney may look a little rough around the edges but in reality it's a quirky haven of original food and novel retail ventures.

Start your walk at ❶ *Violet Cakes*. This cosy California bakery is the creation of Claire Ptak, former pastry chef at Alice Waters' Chez Panisse. Head here for chocolate-wafer-sandwich cookies and Ptak's signature cupcakes, including flavours such as Valrhona chocolate and violet. Next, for a cup of coffee with a sense of theatre, head a couple of doors down to ❷ *Wilton Way Café*, an establishment that offers up avocado and toast and flat

whites to be enjoyed alongside live broadcasts from their in-house radio station, London Fields Radio.

For a spot of shopping, pop your head into ❸ *J Glinert*. Open Thursdays to Sundays, this is the passion project of art technician Tom Budding and stocks a varied selection of products, from Kaweco pens to Terry England pencil clips. A few doors down is ❹ *Momosan Shop*, run by Japanese Momoko Mizutani. You won't find anything run of the mill here; Mizutani has personally scoured the world for unusual and well-designed products. Expect Chemex coffee-makers, *hinoki* wood bath shavings and handmade Finnish clogs.

Head south after you've perused the delights of Wilton Way and, if it's a sunny summer's

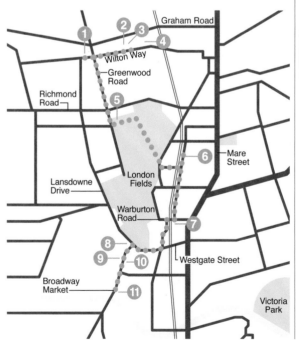

Address book

01 Violet Cakes
47 Wilton Way, E8 3ED
+44 (0)20 7275 8360
violetcakes.com

02 Wilton Way Café
63 Wilton Way, E8 1BG
londonfieldsradio.co.uk

03 J Glinert
71 Wilton Way, E8 1BG
+44 (0)20 7249 6815
jglinert.com

04 Momosan Shop
79A Wilton Way, E8 1BG
momosanshop.com

05 London Fields Lido
London Fields West Side,
E8 3EU
+44 (0)20 7254 9038
better.org.uk

06 E5 Bakehouse
Arch 395 Mentmore
Terrace, E8 3PH
+44 (0)20 8586 9600
e5bakehouse.com

07 London Fields Brewery
365-366 Warburton
Street, E8 3RR
+44 (0)20 7254 7174
londonfieldsbrewery.co.uk

08 Donlon Books
75 Broadway Market,
E8 4PH
+44 (0)20 7684 5698
donlonbooks.com

09 Noble Fine Liquor
27 Broadway Market,
E8 4PH
+44 (0)20 7833 1933
noblefineliquor.co.uk

10 Hill & Szrok
60 Broadway Market,
E8 4QJ
+44 (0)20 7254 8805
hillandszrok.co.uk

11 Peters & Co Gin Palace
F Cooke, 9 Broadway
Market, E8 4PH
+44 (0)7580 691 413
petersginpalace.com

day, wander over to the ⑤ *London Fields Lido* for a cooling dip or a laze on the verdant patch of London Fields. To sample the local culinary culture, make a post-swim stroll over to ⑥ *E5 Bakehouse*, the organic bakery under an old railway arch. Or, for an afternoon pint, sign up for a tour or prop up the bar at ⑦ *London Fields Brewery*, a micro-brewery that has proved instrumental in the city's now-celebrated craft-beer movement. It is located in a former warehouse and you can expect powerfully flavoured Indian Pale Ales, lagers and stouts, as well as jazz music on Sunday nights.

A walk around Hackney wouldn't be complete without an amble down the hipster's sartorial promenade of Broadway Market, which becomes a specialist food market every Saturday. If you can't face the full force of the fashion crowds, head there as close to its 09.00 opening time as you can.

The shops that flank the market are also worth checking out. Lovers of the written word should be sure to visit ⑧ *Donlon Books*, which

specialises in art, photography and music publications. Then there's Climpson & Sons, one of the vanguard of London's recent coffee revolution, and design-conscious wine shop ⑨ *Noble Fine Liquor*, championing small growers.

To end the day, grab a table at ⑩ *Hill & Szrok*. A butcher by day and restaurant by night, this is one of a new breed of young, innovative London butchers sourcing high-quality sustainable meats. The restaurant centres around a shared marble dining table offering cuts of expertly cooked meats from its counter. Get there early or expect to join a long, snaking queue, as they don't take reservations.

And finally, for a slice of East End history, head to traditional pie-and-mash shop F Cooke on the same street. From 19.00 on Thursdays through to Saturdays, this traditional shop transforms into ⑪ *Peters & Co Gin Palace*, a homage to 18th-century gin establishments, once known as "dram shops". It serves 40 types of gin and regular guest varieties.

Getting there

Hackney isn't the most accessible part of London – which is partly why it's still considered a bit unspoiled. Reach Wilton Way on the 277 bus from Highbury and Islington or the 242 from Liverpool Street. Or take the Overground to Hackney Central and walk.

NEIGHBOURHOOD 03

Primrose Hill
City view

Considering the chocolate-box architecture, leafy streets and nearby canal, it is hard to believe that Primrose Hill is within a mile of central London. It is the incongruous nature of this refined urban village – only minutes from the bustling markets of Camden Town to the north and Baker Street to the west yet a world away from the city rat race – that has helped make the picturesque pocket of London one of the capital's most desirable neighbourhoods to live in – and one of its most exclusive.

On any day of the week the action focuses along Regent's Park Road, a street lined with florists, food shops, bookshops and independent boutiques that cuts through the village. On weekends it's the gastropubs dotted across a series of backstreets that soak up the masses.

The prize location (as far as the estate agents of London are concerned) is the spot where a handful of Victorian mansions – reminiscent of dolls' houses, painted in soft whites, pinks, blues, greens and yellows – overlook Regent's Park itself. The view from the tip of the 78-metre-high Primrose Hill is pretty special, too: a cityscape that spans central London to the southeast and Hampstead and Belsize Park to the north.

Stroll in the park
Primrose Hill walk

The main thoroughfare of this well-heeled residential area is Regent's Park Road, a picturesque avenue peppered with a mix of boutiques and family-friendly restaurants. Aspiring chefs should start out here and pop into ❶ *Richard Dare*. This treasure trove of specialist cookware, tableware and kitchen utensils stocks everything from sushi to Sabatier knives.

Turn right off the main street onto Erskine Road and head to ❷ *Press*, where the immaculately dressed women of Primrose Hill tend to shop. It stocks a tightly edited selection of high-fashion womenswear and accessories. Stroll back onto Regent's Park Road and visit ❸ *Lemonia* for a spot of lunch. This family-friendly Greek restaurant is a London institution and has been a convivial local landmark for over 30 years. Expect friendly, familiar service with a dash of Cypriot charm. For sartorial souvenirs

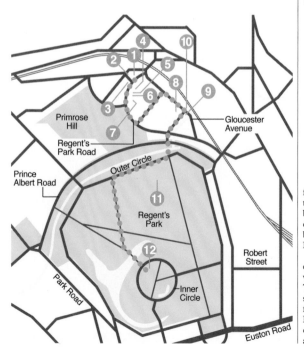

for the little ones, after lunch head to ❹ *Elias and Grace*, a kidswear boutique with an excellent mixture of independent and high-fashion brands that includes Imps and Elves and their own Miller label.

You'll now be ready for an early-afternoon tipple, which is where ❺ *Negozio Classica* comes in. This popular wine bar and shop serves a selection of light Italian food to go with a glass of chianti. But if it's fine dining you're after, cross the street and try to secure a table at ❻ *Odette's*. Open since

Map labels:
Primrose Hill
Regent's Park Road
Prince Albert Road
Outer Circle
Gloucester Avenue
Regent's Park
Robert Street
Park Road
Inner Circle
Euston Road

1978, this intimate neighbourhood restaurant is currently headed by Welsh chef-proprietor Bryn Williams and is great for special occasions. Williams serves classic French cuisine (a throwback to his training under Michel Roux Jr) but favours Welsh ingredients. For more retail therapy, wander over to ❼ *Anna* next. The two-storey womenswear boutique has a loyal following that values owner Anna Park's savvy eye.

Next, catch a breath of fresh air and spectacular views over

London from one of its highest vantage points. Head to the end of Regent's Park Road until you get to the black iron fence that hems in Primrose Hill, the robust patch of hilly green that gives this area its name. Make the short hike to the top and take in the panoramic view of the city that stretches all the way to the dome of St Paul's Cathedral.

When walking back down the hill, cut across the playground to your right and duck down Fitzroy Road. Wander down to the end of the street, turn right and stop off

for a cupcake and cup of tea at ❽ *Primrose Bakery*. Follow that up by settling down (in front of the fire in winter; in the garden in summer) at ❾ *The Engineer* two doors down. This cosy pub has a village-like feel and serves classic pub comfort food in its dining room, bar and pretty back garden. For foodie souvenirs, cross the road to London's smartest delicatessen in the form of ❿ *Melrose and Morgan*. This is a well-designed pantry stocked full of undiscovered food products that draws customers from Primrose Hill and beyond.

You'll now be within striking distance of Regent's Park and the famous ⓫ *ZSL London Zoo*. It's well worth checking the timetable for the zoo's occasional after-hours openings that include wine-tastings and street-food events. In the summer months, culture vultures throng to the ⓬ *Open Air Theatre*, a venue that comes into its own on balmy nights. Catch a spot of Shakespeare then take a stroll north of the park to one of the area's many fine restaurants or wine bars.

Getting there

The best way to get to Primrose Hill is on the Northern line, but you could also get the Overground to Kentish Town West – a 15-minute walk from Regent's Park Road. The 168 bus goes straight to the heart of the area via Bloomsbury and Camden.

Address book

01 Richard Dare
93 Regent's Park Road, NW1 8UR
+44 (0)20 7722 9428

02 Press
3 Erskine Road, NW3 3AJ
+44 (0)20 7449 0081
pressprimrosehill.com

03 Lemonia
89 Regent's Park Road, NW1 8UY
+44 (0)20 7586 7454
lemonia.co.uk

04 Elias and Grace
158 Regent's Park Road, NW1 8XN
+44 (0)20 7449 0574
eliasandgrace.com

05 Negozio Classica
154 Regent's Park Road, NW1 2XN
+44 (0)20 7483 4492
negozioclassica.co.uk

06 Odette's
130 Regent's Park Road, NW1 8XL
+44 (0)20 7586 8569
odettesprimrosehill.com

07 Anna
126 Regent's Park Road, NW1 8XL
+44 (0)20 7483 0411
shopatanna.com

08 Primrose Bakery
69 Gloucester Avenue, NW1 8LD
+44 (0)20 7483 4222
primrose-bakery.co.uk

09 The Engineer
65 Gloucester Avenue, NW1 8JH
+44 (0)20 7483 1890
theengineerprimrosehill. co.uk

10 Melrose and Morgan
42 Gloucester Avenue, NW1 8JD
+44 (0)20 7722 0011
melroseandmorgan.com

11 ZSL London Zoo
Regent's Park, NW1 4RY
+44 (0)344 225 1826
zsl.org

12 Open Air Theatre
Regent's Park, NW1 4NU
+44 (0)844 826 4242
openairtheatre.com

NEIGHBOURHOOD 04
Mayfair
Tailored extravagance

There's a reason why Mayfair occupies the prime location on the London Monopoly board. The neighbourhood lies to the east of the green idylls of Hyde Park and Green Park and is hemmed in to the west by Regent Street, lined with the most expensive retail spaces in the country. It is London's most exclusive area and home to some of the city's most luxurious hotels, shops, restaurants, residences and members' clubs. But there are also lesser-known gems to be found here.

In the heart of Mayfair are the beautiful Berkeley and Grosvenor Squares, named after the aristocratic families who settled here in the 1700s. The latter was declared a public green space in 1946 as part of the peacetime celebrations and is today crowned by the spectacular art deco building of the US Embassy. Further out from the leafy interior, other noteworthy sights are historic hotel Claridge's and the Royal Academy of Arts. Nearby lie Savile Row – best known for its bespoke tailors – the boutiques, galleries and auction houses of New Bond Street and the glamorous private clubs and historic institutions of Piccadilly. Meanwhile, down every street you'll find restaurants, hidden cafés and bustling bars, all suited to the area's well-heeled residents.

Lap of luxury
Mayfair walk

Begin your walk at Bond Street station in the heart of London's West End. Head southeast into South Molton Street, a cosy lane that is lined with pretty shop windows, and stroll past ❶ *Browns*, the peerless fashion store, before ducking into Lancashire Court. Here, you will pass the ❷ *Handel House Museum* at 25 Brook Street, where composer George Frideric Handel lived in the 18th century

and was suitably inspired to compose some of his greatest works.

From here, follow the narrow cobblestone path until it meets Avery Row. Freshen up at ❸ *Ted's Grooming Room* and turn into Brook's Mews, where a rich cup of coffee awaits at ❹ *Taylor Street Baristas*. Around the corner lies Claridge's hotel. If you're here in the evening, stop off at The Fumoir bar, hidden away in the hotel's beautiful art deco interior; the cocktails are the best in town. Turn left and you'll soon arrive at Grosvenor Square, one of London's largest garden squares that was first developed by Sir Richard Grosvenor in 1720.

At the top of the square sits the impressive US Embassy, built by American architect Eero Saarinen in 1938 and capped by an 11-metre-tall gilded aluminium eagle. Past the bronze statue of Ronald Reagan, turn left on to South Audley Street towards Mount Street and you will soon find high-fashion stores including Marc Jacobs, Paule Ka and William & Son.

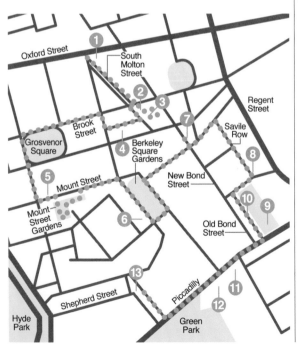

Stop off for a lunch of oysters and fresh fish at the exquisite seafood restaurant ⑤ *Scott's* at number 20 Mount Street, helmed by head chef David McCarthy. At The Connaught hotel turn right towards the lush and peaceful Mount Street Gardens for a short detour before carrying on down Mount Street until Berkeley Square comes into view. This square was named after the first Lord Berkeley and features London's first terraced house: William Kent's 1744-designed number 44, which today houses members' club Annabel's.

The next stop is ⑥ *Maggs Bros*, the 1853-established rare-books and manuscripts dealer. Dive inside for a quick perusal of the antique tomes, cross the plane-tree-lined square and wander down Bruton Place towards New Bond Street. Take in some culture at ⑦ *Halcyon Gallery*, where you'll find Lichtensteins and Warhols, before turning into Conduit Street and then Savile Row, the mecca of bespoke tailoring. Here you'll find heritage brands such as ⑧ *Gieves*

& Hawkes alongside recently refreshed tailor Norton & Sons.

Next, head towards Burlington Gardens, dominated by the impressive façade of the ⑨ *Royal Academy of Arts*. Established in 1768, this is an artist-led gallery that is also home to Britain's first art school. Adjacent to the RA is ⑩ *Burlington Arcade*, said to be the world's first shopping arcade, which will take you to Piccadilly. Once on Piccadilly walk towards Green Park, past ⑪ *The Wolseley* (a café and restaurant in the grand European style, perfect for a lavish breakfast or lunch) and the glinting ⑫ *Ritz* hotel until you reach Halfmoon Street.

From there it's just a quick stroll to Shepherd Market. This charming piazza is surrounded by boutiques and restaurants and is especially romantic during the Christmas season when sparkling lights illuminate the square. Once there, rest your weary legs at ⑬ *Kitty Fisher's* atmospheric British bar and wood-grill restaurant.

Getting there

It's easy to get to Mayfair from any part of London using the Underground. Bond Street is on the Jubilee and Central lines; Oxford Circus is on the Victoria and Bakerloo lines; and Green Park is on the Piccadilly. Avoid buses as Oxford Street gets busy at most times of day.

Address book

01 Browns
24-27 South Molton Street, W1K 5RD
+44 (0)20 7514 0016
brownsfashion.com

02 Handel House Museum
25 Brook Street, W1K 4HB
+44 (0)20 7495 1685
handelhouse.org

03 Ted's Grooming Room
5 Avery Row, W1K 4AL
+44 (0)20 7629 3519
tedsgroomingroom.com

04 Taylor Street Baristas
22 Brook's Mews, W1K 4DY
+44 (0)20 7629 3163
taylor-st.com

05 Scott's
20 Mount Street, W1K 2HE
+44 (0)20 7495 7309
scotts-restaurant.com

06 Maggs Bros
50 Berkeley Square, W1J 5BA
+44 (0)20 7493 7160
maggs.com

07 Halcyon Gallery
144-146 New Bond Street, W1S 2PF
+44 (0)20 7100 7144
halcyongallery.com

08 Gieves & Hawkes
1 Savile Row, W1S 3JR
+44 (0)20 7432 6403
gievesandhawkes.com

09 Royal Academy of Arts
Burlington House, W1J 0BD
+44 (0)20 7300 8000
royalacademy.org.uk

10 Burlington Arcade
51 Piccadilly, W1J 0QJ
+44 (0)20 7493 1764
burlington-arcade.co.uk

11 The Wolseley
160 Piccadilly, W1J 9EB
+44 (0)20 7499 6996
thewolseley.com

12 The Ritz London
150 Piccadilly, W1J 9BR
+44 (0)20 7493 8181
theritzlondon.com

13 Kitty Fisher's
10 Shepherd Market, W1J 7QF
+44 (0)20 3302 1661
kittyfishers.com

NEIGHBOURHOOD 05

Bloomsbury
Georgian architectural elegance

Bloomsbury in central London is one of those districts whose borders are vague. But most would agree that it's focused around lush Russell Square and stretches no further north than Euston Road, nor further east than Gray's Inn Road. It is known for its beautiful terraced Georgian townhouses, picturesque garden squares and village-like atmosphere. The area was first developed by the Russell family in the 18th and early 19th centuries, who laid out the district around squares and built residential houses. Architecturally these Georgian terraces are the most striking aspect of Bloomsbury but there are also a number of brutalist buildings to be found, particularly the Brunswick Centre and the UCL Institute of Education.

Bloomsbury also has a rich cultural history dating back to when Charles Dickens lived here in the 19th century. That said, in literary circles the area is best known for the Bloomsbury Group, an influential set of writers and intellectuals who met here during the early 20th century. Nowadays, Bloomsbury's charm lies in the fact that it is still largely residential and lacks the glass-and-steel office blocks that dominate other parts of the city. In spite of its centrality it hasn't been plagued by foreign buyers and absentee owners and still feels like a lived-in neighbourhood where the residents have a real stake in the place.

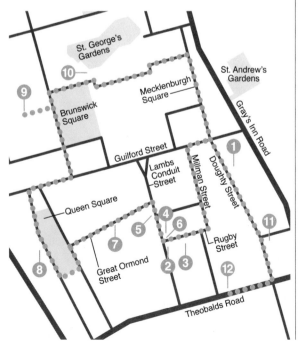

Writers' block
Bloomsbury walk

Start your amble at 48 Doughty Street, a few minutes' walk from Russell Square station, where you will find the ❶*Charles Dickens Museum*. The great novelist lived in this typical Georgian terraced house for only two years, from 1837 to 1839, but managed to write both *Oliver Twist* and *Nicholas Nickleby* in that time. The museum reopened in 2012 after a £3m refurbishment and is home to a number of original artefacts, including Dickens' old writing desk.

From Doughty Street it's a short hop to the shopping district around Lambs Conduit Street. Head first to small side road Rugby Street, where you'll find a few of the capital's best design stores: ❷*Darkroom*, ❸*Pentreath & Hall* and Maggie Owens jewellers. On the part-pedestrianised Lambs Conduit Street there is an interesting mix of high-fashion stores and smaller independent brands' flagships. Top of your list for menswear should be ❹*Private White VC*, Grenson, J.Crew and Oliver Spencer. Meanwhile, bookworms should make a beeline for ❺*Persephone Books*. For lunch, stop off at Spanish restaurant ❻*Cigala* just up the road for simple fish dishes and tapas.

After all that you'll need a hit of caffeine so wander over to ❼*The Espresso Room*, an unassuming kiosk-sized café serving up barista-style coffee opposite London's famous redbrick children's hospital Great Ormond Street. You'll now be within striking

distance of Queen Square, one of Bloomsbury's prettiest garden squares. Look out for the plaque on the floor in the middle of the park marking the site of a bomb explosion during the First World War. As the plaque explains: "Although nearly one thousand people slept in the surrounding buildings, no person was injured." Another highlight of Queen Square is the ⑧ *Art Workers' Guild*, a society for artists and designers housed in a traditional Georgian house and dating back to 1882.

Head north out of Queen Square and wend your way down Grenville Street until you reach ⑨ *The Brunswick Centre*. Retail-wise you won't find much here to inspire you but the building itself is worth noting as one of the best examples of London's brutalist architecture (in the company of the South Bank's National Theatre and the Barbican estate). If you have time, catch a matinee showing at the refurbished Curzon cinema on the east side.

A stone's throw from the Brunswick across the square is

⑩ *The Foundling Museum*, a startling repository of objects from the Foundling Hospital Collection dating back four centuries. Some of the most profound items are the foundling tokens, which mothers pinned to their babies' clothes when they handed them over for care at the hospital's gates. The museum provides a wonderful and quirky look back at the capital's rich history. Here you are also close to the British Museum, which houses a collection of over eight million objects.

To round off your walk you'll need a hearty meal or a cup of tea (depending on the time of day). For a pub lunch of the highest order, retrace your steps to Doughty Street and head to ⑪ *The Lady Ottoline*, which serves up traditional pub grub with a gastro elegance. For a cuppa and something sweet, follow your nose to ⑫ *Bea's of Bloomsbury*, a quaint little neighbourhood café that also houses a cake shop.

Getting there

Russell Square station is at the centre of Bloomsbury and is on the Piccadilly line, which runs through the city centre via Covent Garden and Knightsbridge. The 98 bus terminates here after travelling through Mayfair, while the 188 arrives from the south.

Address book

01 **Charles Dickens Museum**
48 Doughty Street,
WC1N 2LX
+44 (0)20 7405 2127
dickensmuseum.com

02 **Darkroom**
52 Lambs Conduit Street,
WC1N 3LL
+44 (0)20 7831 7244
darkroomlondon.com

03 **Pentreath & Hall**
17 Rugby Street,
WC1N 3QT
+44 (0)20 7430 2526
pentreath-hall.com

04 **Private White VC**
55 Lambs Conduit Street,
WC1N 3NB
+44 (0)20 7831 3344
privatewhitevc.com

05 **Persephone Books**
59 Lambs Conduit Street,
WC1N 3NB
+44 (0)20 7242 9292
persephonebooks.co.uk

06 **Cigala**
54 Lambs Conduit Street,
WC1N 3LW
+44 (0)20 7405 1717
cigala.co.uk

07 **The Espresso Room**
31-35 Great Ormond
Street, WC1N 3HZ
theespressoroom.com

08 **Art Workers' Guild**
6 Queen Square, WC1N 3AT
+44 (0)20 7713 0966
artworkersguild.org

09 **The Brunswick Centre**
WC1N 1BS
+44 (0)20 7833 6066
brunswick.co.uk

10 **The Foundling Museum**
40 Brunswick Square,
WC1N 1AZ
+44 (0)20 7841 3600
foundlingmuseum.org.uk

11 **The Lady Ottoline**
11A Northington Street,
WC1N 2JF
+44 (0)20 7831 0008
theladyottoline.com

12 **Bea's of Bloomsbury**
44 Theobalds Road,
WC1X 8NW
+44 (0)20 7242 8330
beasofbloomsbury.com

Resources
—— Inside
knowledge

So far you've been
inspired by the shops
and the sights, the
galleries and the
gastropubs. But how best
to get there? Herewith a
guide to using London's
labyrinthine transport
system, a source of both
pride and panic among
many Londoners.

This is also the place to
discover the slang, the
soundtrack, the calendar
and the come-rain-or-
shine activities to make
the most of your stay in
the capital, whether
you're here for a good
time or a long time (or
preferably, both).

Transport
Get around town

London has one of the most
extensive transport networks in
the world. Here's a rundown.

01 Underground: Here's how to
get to grips with a London
icon: 1. An Oyster card will
save you time and money
(ask station staff for more
details); 2. Move down inside
the carriage after boarding:
it keeps passive-aggressive
commuters happy; 3. Don't
push the open-door button:
it's redundant.
tfl.gov.uk

02 Bus: London buses have
been given a makeover with
the reintroduction of the
classic Routemaster design
(*see our essay on page 74*).
Use contactless payment for
your journey; it's £1.50 per trip
with Oyster or your bank card.
tfl.gov.uk

03 Bike: Inspired by the
public-bike schemes of our
continental neighbours,
London's bike-friendliness
has vastly improved. "Boris
Bike" rental costs £2 for
24-hour access then £2 per
30-minute period, with the
first 30 minutes free.
tfl.gov.uk

04 Boat: Taking a Thames ferry
will get you from A to B via a
mix of landmarks that make
hardened Londoners swell
with pride. One way is £7.15.
tfl.gov.uk

05 On foot: London's
Underground map can be
deceptive: not all stops are
mapped to scale. Above
ground can be infinitely
better than under.

06 Private car and chauffeur:
For those who prefer a fuss-
free experience, book an
Addison Lee executive car.
addisonlee.com

07 Flights: If you're not flying
commercial there are business
airports close by, including
Farnborough and Biggin Hill.
*tagfarnborough.com;
bigginhillairport.com*

Vocabulary
Local lingo

British self-deprecation is an art
form; play down rather than big
up your grandesse. Cockney
slang may be an anachronism but
the following distilled terminology
might just help a little.

01 Blighty: Great Britain
02 Boozer: pub
03 Boris Bikes: London's
bicycle-rental scheme
04 Fiver: five pounds
05 Loo: toilet
06 Offie: shop selling alcohol
07 Oyster: travel card
08 Pants: underwear
09 Quid: pound
10 Ta: thanks

Soundtrack to the city
Five top tunes

From scene-defining clarion calls
to lyrical paeans to the capital's
charms, download our generation-
spanning London playlist.

01 The Kinks, 'Victoria':
Beyond their beautiful
"Waterloo Sunset", the
Kinks' "Victoria" – all bluesy
riffs and doe-eyed nostalgia
for London's heyday – still
packs a punch.

02 Pet Shop Boys, 'West
End Girls': The electro-pop
pioneers' capital-inspired
1980s classic continues to
fill dancefloors.

03 Eddy Grant, 'Electric
Avenue': Although inspired
by Brixton's riots, this joyous
reggae-tinged hit speaks
volumes of the area's pulse.

04 Amy Winehouse, 'Back
to Black': Camden's most
celebrated songstress's
champagne moment, given
melancholic resonance by
her early demise.

05 The Clash, 'London
Calling': The Joe Strummer-
led punk band's allegiance
to London is confirmed by
the chorus's refrain: "I live
by the river."

Best events
What to see

01 London Collections: Men, various venues: A biannual showcase of the trade's most striking menswear.
January & June, londoncollections.co.uk

02 Boat race, Putney to Mortlake: Oxford University's rowing team takes on Cambridge's in this river-based Battle of Britain.
April, theboatraces.org

03 London Marathon, citywide: The gruelling 26.2-mile loop of the city closes the streets and draws a jubilant crowd.
April, virginmoneylondon marathon.com

04 Wimbledon Championships: The world's premium lawn-tennis competition; Pimm's and strawberries optional.
June-July, wimbledon.org

05 Lovebox Festival, Hackney: A weekend-long celebration of urban music and art.
July, loveboxfestival.com

06 The Proms, Royal Albert Hall: The summertime period when London is serenaded with the world's finest classical music.
July-September, bbc.co.uk/proms

07 London Design Festival, various venues: The city's cutting-edge showcase of contemporary and classic design.
September, londondesignfestival.com

08 Open House London, citywide: London's most fascinating buildings open their doors to the public.
September, openhouselondon.org.uk

09 Frieze London, Regent's Park: The world's leading contemporary-art fair touches down in the capital.
October, friezelondon.com

10 London Film Festival, various venues: Expect thrills, spills and gritty realism at the UK's premier film showcase.
October, bfi.org.uk/lff

Rainy day
Weather-proof activities

Londoners are no strangers to a spot of drizzle but bad weather doesn't spell bad news thanks to the numerous museums and indoor attractions on offer.

01 British Museum: Eight million objects, four wings, more than 250 years of history and zero admission fee. One of the world's most visited sites (and rightly so), the British Museum's commanding, comprehensive exhibits traverse the history of the nation and warrant multiple trips to even begin to get to grips with its scale. Just don't mention the Elgin marbles.
britishmuseum.org

02 Curzon Victoria's film archive: The new HQ for London cinema's most enduring chain, Curzon's Victoria outpost not only features an atmospheric bar and café but a mezzanine level also plays host to a cultural centre where visitors can recline in the leather armchairs and access an extensive archive of films for free, making it the perfect place to while away time between rain showers.
curzoncinemas.com

03 Pub with a log fire: Nothing beats a British boozer (just ask any expat Brit in Sydney what tops their miss-list) and never more so than in winter. Remove the scarf, hat, gloves and coat, grab a fireside stool and make yourself at home at one of the capital's finest hostelries:
The Charles Lamb, Angel
thecharleslambpub.com
The Holly Bush, Hampstead
hollybushhampstead.co.uk
The Palmerston, East Dulwich
thepalmerston.co.uk

(For more pub ideas see Food and drink from page 28)

Sunny day
The great outdoors

On those occasions that the sun does come out, London comes alive. Here are three favourite outdoor excursions.

01 The Southbank: Under the shadow of the towering Shard is London Bridge Station and a spot to start a riverside walk past some of London's cultural flagbearers. Grab a coffee from Borough Market before heading west. Weave through wharves and warehouses until you hit the river, taking in the Tate Modern, Millennium Bridge, Royal Festival Hall, British Film Institute and Hayward Gallery near Waterloo Station. Then cross the bridge to Embankment and head to the atmospheric Gordon's Wine Bar for a cheeseboard.

02 Alfresco swim: The British weather does occasionally heat up and in London there are some excellent spots to swim in the open air. There are a number of beautifully preserved lidos – London Fields, Brockwell and Parliament Hill being just three – plus the tree-lined swimming ponds at Hampstead Heath, also frequented by ducks.

03 River trip to Greenwich: Stretching from Putney in the west to Woolwich in the east, the clipper ferries that traverse the Thames stop up and down the length of the river. Expect spectacular views as the city's chequered history unfolds. Gilded bridges, gleaming skyscrapers and repurposed warehouses stand out en route to historic Greenwich. Here the preserved and restored *Cutty Sark* – one of the original tea clippers – awaits your arrival ahead of a leisurely exploration of Greenwich's Market, Royal Observatory and – an essential – the Meantime Brewery.

About Monocle
—— Take a look around

In 2007, Monocle was launched as a monthly magazine briefing on global affairs, business, culture, design and much more. We believed there was a globally minded audience of readers that were hungry for opportunities and experiences beyond their national borders.

Today Monocle is a complete media brand with print, audio and online elements – not to mention our expanding retail network and online business. Besides our London HQ we have seven international bureaux in New York, Toronto, Istanbul, Singapore, Tokyo, Zürich and Hong Kong. We continue to grow and flourish and at our core is the simple belief that there will always be a place for a print brand that is committed to telling fresh stories and sending photographers on assignments. It's also a case of knowing that our success is all down to the readers, advertisers and collaborators who have supported us along the way.

Park life
Our HQ abuts Paddington Street Gardens

① Print
Quality and quantity

MONOCLE is published 10 times a year out of our HQ in London. We have stayed loyal to our belief in quality print with two new seasonal publications: THE FORECAST, packed with key insights into the year ahead, and THE ESCAPIST, our summer travel-minded magazine which also delivers business ideas. Since 2013 we have also had a book collaboration with publisher Gestalten.

On air
—
Our radio studios are on site at Midori House

(2)
Radio
Sound approach

Monocle 24 is our round-the-clock radio station that launched in 2011. The station delivers global news and shows covering foreign affairs, urbanism, business, culture, design, print media and food and drink. We also have a playlist to accompany you day and night, regularly assisted by live sessions that are hosted at our very own Midori House.

(3)
Online
Digital delivery

We also have a dynamic website: *monocle.com*. As well as being the place to hear Monocle 24 – or, if you are a subscriber, have access to all the stories ever run in the magazine – we use the site to present our films. Beautifully shot and edited by our in-house team, these films provide a fresh perspective on stories reflecting our editorial philosophy.

(4)
Retail and cafés
Good taste

Via our shops in New York, London, Toronto, Hong Kong, Tokyo and Singapore we sell products that cater to our readers' tastes and are produced in collaboration with brands we believe in. We also have cafés in Tokyo and London serving Japanese delicacies and reviving coffee – and we are set to expand this arm of our business.
monocle.com/shop; cafe.monocle.com

Writers
Mikaela Aitken
Matt Alagiah
Steve Bloomfield
Robert Bound
Pete Brown
Tom Edwards
Josh Fehnert
Nelly Gocheva
Tom Hall
Markus Hippi
Alicia Kirby
Jason Li
Hugo Macdonald
David Michon
Tom Morris
Paul Noble
Ben Olsen
David Plaisant
Thomas Reynolds
Chiara Rimella
Marie-Sophie Schwarzer
Richard Spencer Powell
Andrew Tuck

Chief photographer
Andrew Urwin

Still life
Anders Gramer
David Sykes

Photographers
Max A Rush
Marc Atkins
Jonathan Birch
Michael Bryant
Helen Cathcart
Addie Chinn
Tom Cronin
Ana Cuba
Dennis Gilbert
John Hammond
Peter Heppelwhite
Britta Jaschinski
Stefan Johnson
Steven Joyce
Toby Keane
Stuart Leech
Jayne Lloyd
David Loftus
Marcus Mac Innes
Ray Main
Benjamin McMahon
Trent McMinn
Andrew Meredith
Rafal Motkovicz
Patricia Niven
Felix Odell
Ben Quinton
Paul Raeside
Chris Ridley
Damien Russell
Durston Saylor
Jefferson Smith
Chalky Whyte
Paul Winch-Furness
Gary Wolff

Illustrators
Satoshi Hashimoto
Tokuma
Masao Yamazaki

CHAPTER EDITING

Ⓜ
Need to know
Andrew Tuck

Ⓗ ❶
Hotels
Josh Fehnert

Ⓕ ❷
Food and drink
Josh Fehnert
Alicia Kirby

Ⓡ ❸
Retail
Nelly Gocheva

Ⓣ ❹
Things we'd buy
Nelly Gocheva

Ⓔ ❺
Essays
Nelly Gocheva

Ⓒ ❻
Culture
Robert Bound

Ⓓ ❼
Design and architecture
Tom Morris
David Plaisant

Ⓢ ❽
Sport and fitness
Matt Alagiah

Ⓦ ❾
Walks
Matt Alagiah
Alicia Kirby

Ⓜ

Resources
Ben Olsen

Research
Mikaela Aitken
Stefano Fumagalli
Alia Massoud
Henry Rees-Sheridan
Chiara Rimella
Marie-Sophie Schwarzer
Alex Stenbock-Fermor

Special thanks
Richard Dennis
Paul Fairclough
Lee Gale
Tom Hall
Maria Hamer
Anthony Pearce
Beatrice Prokofiev
Adam Richmond

Monocle
EDITOR IN CHIEF & CHAIRMAN
Tyler Brûlé
EDITOR
Andrew Tuck

**The Monocle Travel Guide
Series: London**
EDITOR
Nelly Gocheva

DESIGNER
Jay Yeo

PHOTO EDITORS
Lois Wright
Alex Wheeler
Poppy Shibamoto

PRODUCTION
Jacqueline Deacon
Dan Poole
Ben Olsen

We hope you have found the Monocle travel guide to London useful, informative, inspiring and entertaining – and continue to do so for years to come. There is plenty more to get your teeth into: you'll also find our New York guide on shelves now, with Tokyo and Hong Kong coming soon. Cities are fun. Let's explore.

01

London

The sights, sounds and style of the British capital.

02

New York

From the bright neon lights to the moody jazz clubs of the US's starring city.

03

Tokyo

Japan's capital in all its energetic, enigmatic glory.

04

Hong Kong

Get down to business in this vibrant city of depth and drama.